THE ART OF TAX REPRESENTATION

FELECIA G DIXSON EA, CTRC, ATA
ENROLLED AGENT, CERTIFIED TAX REPRESENTATION CONSULTANT,
ACCREDITED TAX ADVISOR

IRS Tax Representation
“Don’t go Alone.”

By

Felecia Gail Dixson, EA, CTRC, ATA

Enrolled Agent

Certified Tax Representation Consultant

Accreted Tax Advisor

The Art of Tax Representation:
Tax Representation Don't Go Alone

Veritas Ink and Press is committed to excellence in the publishing Industry.

Published in the United States of America

ISBN: 979-8-3493-0950-2
eISBN: 979-8-3493-0951-9

ACKNOWLEDGEMENT & DEDICATION

To my family, none of this would be possible.

To my life partner, Kenny,

Thank you for your constant, unwavering support.

Your presence has been a steady light, and I am grateful for every step we take together.

To my beloved daughter, Felecia Annette

Thank you for your unwavering support and understanding as you grew into an incredible person by my side. For the many missed vacation trips and endless nights, I practiced being a good mom as well as the best Tax Professional that I could be

Your love and resilience have been a true gift, and I am endlessly grateful.

To my wonderful parents, Nancy and Roy Skiles

For instilling in me the invaluable business principles that have guided me throughout my career and life.

Your wisdom and encouragement laid the foundation for my journey.

To my TRN Network family,

Thank you for your support and camaraderie.

You have played a part in my growth, and your kindness will always be cherished.

To my Faith

I thank God for giving me the strength and knowledge to help others in their time of need.

REVIEWS

Felecia is terrific with clients and understands the ins and outs of tax resolution. She is the consummate professional and someone I cannot recommend enough!

Eric Green, Esq. Tax Attorney

If you want a tax consultant who's as dynamic as a Disney dancer, explosive as a fireworks display engineer, and harmonious as a Nashville singer, look no further than Felcia Dixson. She's not just your run-of-the-mill tax expert – she's a powerhouse of talent and dedication. With her background in entertaining crowds and her commitment to serving veterans, Felecia brings a unique perspective to tax matters. Her expertise in military tax issues is unmatched, making her the go-to person for tax questions. Unsurprisingly, she's earned her spot as one of TaxBuzz's Top 100 professionals. Felecia Dixson is your undeniable choice when you need tax resolution with a touch of showbiz flair and a heart for those who served.

Carlos Samaniego, EA, NTPI Fellow

Felecia Dixson is a fellow national trainer with Tax Rep LLC. She has an amazing temperament when helping people resolve their tax issues. She cares and listens carefully to what the client has to say. She also crafts a plan to resolve the tax issue and informs her clients of progress. If you need tax representation - you can't do any better than Felecia.

Patrick H. Wanzer, CPA, CTRC

I have had the pleasure of working with Felecia through our mutual interest in tax representation, and she has consistently proven to be a fantastic professional. Her deep knowledge and years of experience in tax controversy make her an invaluable asset on any project. Felecia's thoroughness and attention to detail are unmatched, and I frequently reach out to her for a second opinion when I encounter complex issues. Her ability to navigate challenging tax situations and help clients achieve positive outcomes is a testament to her expertise and dedication.

Rayath Chowdhury, CPA

Table of Contents

Chapter 1: Bad Things Happen to Good People Every Day.

"Our new Constitution is now established, everything seems to promise it will be durable; but, in this world, nothing is certain except death and taxes."

— Benjamin Franklin

The above statement is one of the most quoted ones in the USA and even in other countries. The concept of certainty of paying taxes was not new at the time, but Franklin's words made it immortal. The beauty of this quote is that it holds true to date and will, I believe, remain so for eternity. And why not, by the way? After all, taxes and finances are the things I do every day. Well, I'm going to do the same thing in this book, too, to help you come out of the bad tax financial hole.

Before we delve into a detailed account of the topic of this book, let me assure you that it is going to be a life-changing read... for the better, of course. Having read this book, dealing with your taxes and the IRS will give you no more nightmares.

Hi, I'm Felecia, and I'm your Certified Tax Representation Consultant. I can help you resolve your tax-related worries and I can help make the IRS stop chasing you.

Undeniably, the IRS is a constant guest, and you must entertain this guest; there is no escape from this department. Why? Because one of the core purposes of the IRS is to collect taxes and let me assure you here that they are very good at doing it, no matter what.

If you owe taxes, you will find them standing right in front of you or behind you. Simply put, you will be surrounded by them.

The thing we need to clearly understand here is that you are not taxed until your wealth and income enter into your due tax bracket. If not, you will not find the IRS anywhere near you. So, it makes a simple equation:

Taxable Income & Wealth = Due tax must be paid

No Taxable Income & Wealth = NO TAX to be paid

Well, isn't it some great news? I mean, no taxes. To be honest, nobody would like to be in the non-taxed bracket because it also means no money.

Well, the IRS Revenue Officers and Agents are indeed smart and have made the structure in a way that almost no one can escape from being taxed… until you are not in the United States. So, now understand this delicate point here; the equation above signifies that you must have enough money to attract to be taxed and that your taxes are never more than your income and overall wealth you possess.

Now, the real question arises:

"Why do people still fall into the bad tax financial hole when they are taxed only for the wealth they already have?"

If you notice, you will find that people struggling to pay their taxes are all good people and have no intention of escaping from their liabilities and duties. They are all willing to go by the book, yet they find themselves falling deeper into the bad tax financial hole, even when they have enough resources. This is when I say, "Bad Things Happen to Good People Every Day." On the bright side, I know for a fact that "Good People Overcome Bad Things Every Day."

And you are, I know, good people!

Overcoming bad things is all about making a proper, detailed plan, which I will expose in this book how you, too, can make this possible. But before that, we need to understand why it all happens that the IRS has to come after you. On the contrary, I analyze my clients' issues and bring them the best IRS resolutions possible.

Now, let me show you the reasons and IRS tax resolutions with real-life scenarios. Let's see a few reasons first:

Under-Withholding

Employers are required to deduct taxes from your wages by law. However, it might not be widely known that if your wages have insufficient tax withheld over the course of the year, you, as the employee, might end up owing money to the IRS at the time of filing your tax return. This situation is referred to as "under-withholding."[1]

This often occurs when an employee claims too many exemptions on their IRS Form W-4, which is filled out upon employment commencement. As a result, an inadequate amount of income tax is deducted from their earnings throughout the year.

Should you discover that too much tax has been withheld, it's possible to adjust this by submitting a new W-4 form at any time. Doing so can ensure that any overpayment is refunded when you submit your annual income tax return.

Unaccounted Income

With the increase in the gig economy, people are now earning from various sources, which can make tracking income challenging. This situation can result in unexpected tax bills. Not reporting all income sources, particularly for freelancers or those with multiple income streams, can cause issues with taxes. Moreover, freelancers are required to cover the full 15.3% of Medicare and Social Security taxes, unlike traditional employees who share this cost with their employers.

Complexity of Tax Documentation

Not filing tax returns is a common yet highly problematic concern that leads to tax complications. Often, individuals avoid

---

[1] https://www.investopedia.com/terms/u/underwithholding.asp

filing their taxes because they find the process daunting or overwhelming.

In cases where filing involves intricate paperwork, such as tax returns with numerous forms and supporting documents, individuals may become overwhelmed by the complexity, and it can lead to delays as they struggle to gather and organize the necessary information.

Financial Challenges

Financial difficulties can significantly impact your ability to meet filing deadlines. Businesses facing financial constraints may prioritize immediate operational needs over compliance tasks, resulting in delayed filings.

For many families, the budget is stretched so thin that there are insufficient funds to cover tax liabilities. Financial setbacks, unforeseen expenses, or changes in job circumstances can make it challenging to fulfill tax commitments.

In the case of small businesses and families with limited resources, they may face challenges in dedicating time and personnel to manage filing responsibilities. This can lead to unintentional delays, especially if there is a reliance on a single person for filing tasks.

Busy Schedules and Overlooked Deadlines

Tax obligations are sometimes neglected by individuals who are juggling busy schedules, with immediate concerns taking precedence over settling debts with the IRS. The pressures of work, family life, and other duties can lead to postponement or oversight of tax responsibilities.

Technological Challenges

In an era where many filings are done electronically, technological barriers can contribute to delinquency. This is particularly true for people in the advanced age group. Lack of access to reliable internet, computer issues, or unfamiliarity with digital filing systems can impede timely submissions.

Errors Due to Confusion

Delinquency may also arise from miscommunication or misunderstanding of filing requirements. The complexity and constant updates of the tax code make it difficult, often leading to errors in tax filings. Misunderstandings about tax regulations, deductions, or credits can cause you to file incorrectly. Here, you can see the importance of seeking help from a tax professional for any questions or uncertainties about tax matters.

In a similar vein, people simply lack awareness. They may be unaware of filing requirements or deadlines. This lack of awareness can result from changes in regulations, updated procedures, or a failure to stay informed about evolving compliance obligations. Staying in contact with a tax professional can help you deal with this reason.

Procrastination

One of the most common reasons for being delinquent in filing is simple procrastination. Individuals or businesses may delay filing due to a lack of organization, time constraints, or a belief that the deadline is further away than it actually is.

Change in Personal Circumstances

If you are going through a major life change, such as a divorce, death in the family, or relocation, you may find it challenging to focus on administrative tasks like filing. These significant life events can disrupt regular routines and lead to unintentional filing delays. Businesses also face similar challenges when they are up against unforeseen challenges like a sudden decline in the customer base or a saturated market, among others.

As you can see, being delinquent in filing can result from a combination of personal, organizational, and circumstantial factors. Recognizing these reasons is crucial for implementing proactive strategies to address and prevent filing delays. Whether through better organization, increased awareness, or leveraging available resources, you can take steps to enhance your filing processes and maintain compliance with the IRS's regulatory obligations.

What if you don't pay your taxes?

Failing to make a tax payment can lead to the forfeiture of any expected refund. However, the repercussions extend far beyond if you have a tax debt.

Case Study: Thomas Abernathy

Thomas Abernathy is a 45-year-old software developer, and he found himself in a precarious financial situation because of multiple years of unfiled taxes. Despite a successful career, his financial literacy was limited, a gap that became glaringly evident as he faced the consequences of tax delinquency. Living in a suburban area with his spouse and two children, his life is typical of many middle-class Americans, juggling mortgage payments, education expenses, and the costs of daily living.

Financial Profile of Thomas Abernathy

- **Occupation:** Senior Software Developer
- **Annual Income:** $120,000
- **Family Status:** Married with two children
- **Living Situation:** Homeowner with a mortgage
- **Unfiled Tax Years:** 3 years
- **Estimated Unpaid Taxes:** $45,000

The path to Thomas's tax delinquency was not a result of deliberate evasion but a combination of factors that, over time, created a significant barrier to compliance. He is a good person, but bad things did happen to him.

Thomas's expertise in software development did not translate into financial savvy. His understanding of tax obligations, deductions, and the importance of timely filing was limited. This lack of knowledge led to procrastination and, ultimately, to the failure to file.

During the years in question, Thomas faced several personal challenges, including a serious illness in the family and the subsequent financial strain from medical bills. These events diverted his attention and resources away from tax obligations, contributing to his delinquency.

So far, does it sound familiar? Yes, I know it does!

So, as time passed, the fear of potential penalties, interest charges, and the complexity of resolving his tax situation became paralyzing for him. This fear, compounded by his lack of knowledge on how to address the issue, led to further inaction.

Recognizing the severity of his situation, Thomas sought professional help to resolve his tax delinquency. The pathway to resolution involved several key steps, with which we facilitated him.

The first step involved a detailed assessment of Thomas's financial situation, identifying all unfiled tax years and estimating the total tax liability. This phase included gathering all necessary documentation and filing the overdue returns, a process known as becoming compliant with the IRS.

Given the amount owed, Thomas was not in a position to pay the full sum immediately. We negotiated an installment agreement with the IRS, allowing Thomas to pay his tax debt over time in manageable monthly payments. This agreement considered

Thomas's current financial situation, ensuring that the payment plan was realistic and sustainable.

To reduce the financial burden, we filed for a penalty abatement, citing reasonable cause due to the family medical crisis. By providing detailed documentation of the circumstances that led to his tax delinquency, Thomas was able to have some of the penalties reduced, decreasing his overall debt.

Thomas Abernathy's journey from tax delinquency to financial stability shows the complexities and emotional toll of tax issues. It also showcases the potential for IRS resolutions and recovery through informed actions and professional assistance. By engaging us to address his tax delinquency head-on and committing to financial education, Thomas was able to restore his fiscal health and set a course for a secure financial future.

You can see the importance of financial literacy, the benefits of seeking professional guidance in tax matters, and the IRS's willingness to work with taxpayers to resolve outstanding obligations. Tax problems can be daunting, but they are not undefeatable, and the path to IRS resolution is accessible with the right professional support and resources.

Case Study: Sarah Walter

Sarah Walter is the owner of a small business; it is a small digital marketing and web design business established five years ago. Her company has grown from a solo operation to employing ten full-time employees. The business serves a diverse clientele, offering services ranging from website development to digital marketing campaigns.

Business Profile

- **Business Name: Walter's Digi World**
- **Owner: Sarah Walter**
- **Industry: Digital Marketing and Web Design**

- **Location: San Francisco, California**
- **Number of Employees: 10**
- **Years in Operation: 5**
- **Annual Revenue: $600,000**
- **Unpaid Payroll Taxes Period: 2 years**

Sarah's failure to pay payroll taxes was not a result of willful neglect but stemmed from a series of misunderstandings and unforeseen challenges.

Sarah experienced rapid growth, which brought about significant cash flow management challenges. She, focusing on expanding her business, inadvertently overlooked the importance of setting aside sufficient funds for payroll taxes.

With a background in web design and digital marketing, Sarah possessed limited knowledge of financial management and tax compliance, which led to the mismanagement of funds allocated for payroll taxes.

Sarah's business encountered unexpected expenses, including the urgent need for new equipment and software upgrades. These expenses consumed a large portion of the operating budget, leaving insufficient funds for payroll taxes.

Sarah had outsourced her payroll and accounting functions to a third-party service provider. Unfortunately, miscommunications regarding the scope of services led to the assumption that the provider was handling payroll tax payments, which was not the case.

Upon recognizing the severity of her situation, Sarah took proactive steps to address and resolve the unpaid payroll taxes. The resolution process involved several strategic actions.

When Sarah got in touch with us, we conducted a thorough review of her financial records, determined the total amount of unpaid payroll taxes, and developed a plan for resolution.

We initiated contact with the IRS to explain the situation and express Sarah's intent to resolve the unpaid taxes. Open and honest communication was key to establishing trust and cooperation with the IRS.

Given the amount owed, paying the full sum immediately was not possible for Sarah. We negotiated an installment agreement with the IRS, allowing the business to pay back the owed taxes over an agreed-upon period. This plan was designed to be realistic, considering the company's monthly cash flow and operational expenses.

Recognizing that Sarah's failure to pay payroll taxes was not due to willful neglect, we filed for a penalty abatement, citing reasonable cause based on the miscommunication with Sarah's previous accounting service and unexpected business expenses. This request aimed to reduce the overall financial burden by eliminating some of the penalties accrued.

To prevent future payroll tax issues, we helped Sarah implement proven financial management practices. We asked her to conduct monthly reviews of the business's financial status, including cash flow, expenses, and tax obligations.

Just like Sarah, a number of small business owners face challenges in managing payroll taxes and end up with unpaid payroll taxes. Through proactive steps, honest communication with the IRS, and the implementation of sound financial management practices, Sarah resolved her unpaid payroll taxes and set her business on a path to financial stability.

Since we are talking about unpaid payroll taxes here, let me share some important details.

Payroll taxes consist of funds deducted from employees' salaries to support Medicare and Social Security programs. These are also known as FICA taxes, an acronym for the Federal

Insurance Contributions Act, which established these contributions.

The discrepancy between taxes owed and those actually paid to the IRS is referred to as the tax gap. A portion of this gap includes employment taxes not paid by some business owners who fell behind. However, there are instances where the shortfall is a result of deliberate deceit. To combat employment tax fraud, the Tax Division of the Department of Justice collaborates closely with the IRS and U.S. Attorneys, seeking financial penalties, legal injunctions, and criminal charges against offenders.

Do the people in these case studies sound familiar? Aren't they good people? Indeed, they are, but bad things happened to them. There are a lot more people like them who are stuck in this bad tax financial hole, but not forever, provided that they are ready to come out of it, just like Thomas and Sarah. Rest assured that help is always available and is just a phone call away.

Remember that no institution, and certainly not the IRS, has been founded at random. It takes years of research and planning and a period of trial and error to establish an institution. Yes, it is planning at the core that always works. And that's what tax professionals do at their best. You need to realize that engaging a professional is not a choice but a dire need of yours today in order to come out of the bad tax financial hole and stay out of it for the rest of your life. Once you are with a professional, you will find IRS resolutions that always work for sure.

As I discussed above, a delay in seeking professional help can have dire consequences on your financial and emotional health.

Delinquency in tax filing will trap you in a cycle of increasing debt, growing tax liabilities, and mounting legal challenges. It's a nightmare that many find themselves in when financial hardships spiral out of control.

The fear of drowning in debt, facing the IRS, and fighting legal battles is real, and the longer you wait, the direr the situation becomes.

Today, for you, professional help is not a luxury but a necessity for your financial recovery and further stability. Taking this step will mitigate the adverse effects of current as well as future financial challenges.

When you do it alone in the confusing world of taxes, all you can experience are fines, penalties, and really frightening legal issues.

The tax rules are always changing, and tax experts such as myself are the ones who work hard to stay updated with these changes so that they can keep you safe from tax and financial nightmares. It's not just about following the law; it's crucial for keeping your money healthy. Not following the rules can have grave consequences, and that's something you definitely want to avoid.

The longer you wait, the worse your problems can get.

Tax professionals aren't just there to fix immediate problems; we are like guides who also help you plan for the future, avoiding unpleasant surprises and making the most of the available opportunities in the always-changing world of finances. We are the key to your financial freedom and stability. Don't let fear stop you; let it be the reason you take a step toward a better, safer future.

Now is the right time to call a tax professional if you want to move with absolute peace of mind.

Seeking professional help is not a show of weakness but rather of wisdom and forethought. We, the professionals, can provide you with optimal financial outcomes for sure. As a result, you will be able to move forward to a future of informed decisions and lasting financial stability.

Chapter 2: What Happens If I Don't Have the Money to Pay the IRS?

Managing tax obligations can feel crushing, especially when you find yourself in the uncomfortable position of owing more to the IRS than you can afford to pay.

Well, it is a common challenge many face, but with the right approach, it can be managed smoothly.

Recognizing the issue early and timely addressing it is the key to preventing problems from growing into larger ones.

In this chapter, I'll show you what options you have and how to take effective action swiftly to avoid the accumulation of penalties and interest when you don't have enough money at hand to pay the IRS.

Let me tell you that facing tax debt is common. Being a professional in this field, I meet such people daily, and I provide them with my time-tested strategies to help manage the tax burden.

Remember that there are certain consequences of delayed payment, but you can take steps with various relief options when it comes to dealing with the IRS.

With a clearer understanding of the processes, if you have unpaid taxes, you'll be better prepared to handle your tax obligations confidently and make informed decisions to arrange the money to pay your taxes.

So, first of all, let's see what happens if you have unpaid taxes; it all starts with the notices from the IRS.

The IRS sends a series of notices to alert you of your unpaid taxes. Initially, you may receive a CP14 notice, a polite reminder of your tax debt.

If unpaid, the IRS escalates to a CP501 notice, signaling more urgency for you to address the debt.

Ignoring CP14 and CP501 can lead to a CP2000 notice, which indicates a grave concern for you with dire consequences.

Each notice marks a progression into deeper tax compliance issues.

When you don't pay your taxes, several penalties and consequences follow. By the way, these consequences impact not just your finances but your personal and professional life, too.

Firstly, a failure-to-pay penalty of 0.5% per month on the unpaid tax amount is imposed, capped at 25%. Interest also accrues from the due date until full payment, compounding daily at the federal short-term rate plus 3%. This means that you now have to pay extra when you don't have enough money to begin with!

The IRS may also file a federal tax lien against your property, which harms your credit score and restricts property transactions. For more severe cases, the IRS can levy your assets, including bank accounts and wages.

If your tax debt exceeds $54,000, the IRS may revoke your passport, restricting international travel. So now, not only are you left with a huge amount of debt to pay off, but you are also restricted from traveling internationally, should you have to for any reason!

Future tax refunds you might be entitled to can also be intercepted to offset your debt.

In extreme cases, unpaid taxes can escalate to charges of tax evasion, leading to rigorous investigations. If proven, penalties include hefty fines and possible jail time.

When faced with the realization that you can't pay your due taxes, you need to act promptly and strategically.

Begin by reviewing your tax return to confirm the amount you owe. This includes not only the principal amount but also any penalties and interest already accrued. If you're unsure about the calculations or the items included in your tax bill, seek help from a tax professional.

Errors can occur in tax assessments. Ensure that every income statement, deduction, and credit has been accurately reported and calculated. If you discover discrepancies, address these issues with the IRS or consult a tax advisor for guidance on how to proceed.

Contacting the IRS may seem daunting, but it's a necessary step. Inform them of your financial situation and express your willingness to settle your debts.

However, it is tricky to initiate communication with the IRS. At this stage, accompanying a CPA, EA, or tax attorney is advised to talk on your behalf.

After notifying the IRS about your situation, we can discuss the possible payment options that we figure out. The payment options can range from short-term extensions to more structured payment plans.

We keep detailed records of all communications with the IRS, including dates and the names of the representatives we speak with. This documentation is invaluable in case of misunderstandings or disputes.

With my team, I have helped a number of people in managing their taxes when they didn't have enough money to pay the IRS.

We have helped people in situations when they thought they had no other option but to face a lien or levy or get their passports revoked.

Let's see a few case studies where people were desperate and struggling to get the IRS out of their hair. However, with our expertise in tax management, they faced no penalties.

Case Study: Jason Edward's IRS Tax Debt

Jason Edward, a freelance graphic designer, encountered a financial difficulty when he realized he was unable to pay his owed taxes for the past year.

His income was irregular, and unexpected personal expenses had significantly reduced his savings. This left Jason with no money for his tax liabilities and facing potential penalties and interest that could further worsen his financial burden.

Without timely intervention, the situation could escalate to more severe consequences, such as tax liens or levies on his property and assets.

To address this situation, our first step was to initiate communication with the IRS, informing them of Jason's financial struggles and his commitment to resolving his tax debt.

This proactive approach helped prevent the immediate imposition of additional penalties. We also conducted a thorough review of Jason's tax returns to ensure all income was accurately reported and that he received all the deductions and credits he was entitled to. This was crucial to determine the precise amount of the tax debt.

Recognizing Jason's limited financial capacity, we negotiated an Installment Agreement with the IRS, allowing him to pay off his tax debt over time in smaller, manageable payments.

The arrangement of the Installment Agreement helped Jason avoid overwhelming financial strain. Additionally, we applied for penalty abatement on Jason's behalf, considering his previous good standing with the IRS and the unexpected financial hardships that led to his inability to pay. This aimed to reduce the overall burden by eliminating some of the penalties accrued on his tax debt.

We also provided Jason with professional advice on budget management and financial planning. This guidance was essential for him to understand how to better manage his finances and prevent future tax issues.

Discussions on adjusting his tax withholdings and making quarterly estimated tax payments were also part of our strategy to align his payments with his fluctuating income.

We scheduled regular follow-ups to monitor Jason's compliance with the payment plan and any new IRS requirements. This ongoing support ensured that he remained on track and made necessary adjustments to his financial planning strategies.

Ultimately, through the Installment Agreement, Jason was able to fully pay off his tax debt within the negotiated timeframe without additional financial strain.

At one time, Jason had unpaid taxes, but he had no money at all to settle the debt. In the first place, our intervention prevented further penalties and stopped the progression toward more severe consequences like liens or levies.

Secondly, knowing that he couldn't afford to pay immediately, we opted for a solution that bought him enough time to arrange sufficient funds.

Thirdly, with our financial advice, Jason improved his budgeting skills and gained better control over his financial situation, significantly reducing the likelihood of future tax issues.

By addressing the problem early, communicating openly with the IRS, and establishing a realistic payment plan, you can overcome financial challenges and achieve compliance with their tax obligations, especially when you have no funds at hand.

Case Study: Sarah Thompson's Fear of Losing Her Assets

Sarah Thompson, a small business owner specializing in organic skin care products, found herself in a tight spot when she realized that she could not pay her taxes due to a downturn in business caused by unexpected market shifts.

Her situation was compounded by significant inventory costs, which tied up much of her available cash.

Sarah was anxious about the potential for accruing penalties and the possibility of more severe IRS actions if her tax debts remained unpaid. She never missed paying her taxes, and the thought of not paying the due taxes on time scared her.

Sarah feared losing her business and property because she had this idea of levy. When she met us, she was almost certain that the IRS would take her assets since she had no funds.

Recognizing the urgency of her situation, our first step was to accurately assess her total tax liability by reviewing her latest tax returns. This ensured that all possible deductions had been claimed and that there were no errors in the tax amount due.

Once we had a clear picture of her financial obligations, we promptly initiated a dialogue with the IRS, explaining Sarah's current financial difficulties and her intention to resolve the outstanding tax debt. We showed her previous records that she never missed paying her taxes.

Given the nature of Sarah's cash flow issues, we explored several relief options with the IRS.

After a detailed analysis of her financial situation, we decided that requesting a short-term extension to pay would be the most feasible solution. This extension provided Sarah with additional time to pay her taxes without incurring significant penalties.

Simultaneously, we arranged for a partial payment installment agreement, which allowed her to start making payments based on her current financial capability, thereby demonstrating her commitment to fulfilling her tax obligations.

To further assist Sarah in managing her financial challenges, we helped her restructure her business budget, focusing on reducing non-essential expenses and optimizing inventory management.

Our budgeting advice turned out to be crucial in improving her cash flow, making it more feasible for her to meet her installment payments and future tax liabilities.

In addition to the restructuring, we implemented a system for better financial tracking and planning within her business. This system helped Sarah forecast her earnings and expenses more accurately, which was essential for maintaining her financial health and preventing future tax issues.

We also advised her to adjust her quarterly tax payments to better reflect her current earnings, thereby avoiding the accumulation of tax debt in the future.

Throughout this process, we maintained regular contact with Sarah, providing ongoing support and ensuring she adhered to the agreed payment plans and IRS regulations.

Our consistent monitoring and guidance helped Sarah not only manage her tax debt effectively but also placed her business on a more stable financial footing.

As a result of these concerted efforts, Sarah was able to fulfill her tax obligations without incurring further debt, and her business returned to profitability.

We did it all for Sarah when she had no funds and even thought of losing what she had.

At this point, let me tell you that fearing and worrying will never bring you a solution.

Now, who can bring a solution?

Yes, an expert in the field can… for sure!

Case Study: Strategic Asset Liquidation for Jake and Linda

Jake and Linda, a retired couple, found themselves facing a $15,000 tax bill from the IRS.

As retirees, they were concerned about the financial impact this liability would have on their fixed income. So, they sort of had no money to pay their taxes.

They needed a solution that would resolve their tax issues without compromising their long-term financial security. They reached out for professional guidance to explore their options and mitigate the financial impact of their tax debt.

Upon reviewing Jake and Linda's financial situation, it was clear that their income was insufficient to cover their due taxes without affecting their standard of living. This situation was quite challenging for us as well.

As we discussed further, we found out that they owned a piece of non-income-producing land. They told us that they didn't want to sell it as they had an emotional attachment to it.

After a thorough assessment of their assets, we determined that liquidating the non-income-producing land was a viable solution.

We explained to them that liquidating would allow them to pay off their tax bill in full, avoiding the accumulation of interest and penalties that would further strain their finances.

Our goal was to ensure that the sale of the land would be handled strategically to maximize the return and minimize any potential drawbacks.

We guided Jake and Linda through the process of selling their land.

We assessed the current market value of the land to ensure it was sold at an optimal price and calculated any potential capital gains tax that could arise from the sale and planning strategies to minimize its impact.

We coordinated with real estate professionals to facilitate the sale and ensure all legal and financial processes were handled efficiently.

The land was successfully sold, and the proceeds from the sale covered the $15,000 tax bill in full.

Jake and Linda were relieved to resolve their tax debt without incurring further financial hardship. The careful consideration of the sale's timing and conditions ensured that they received a favorable price for their property, which ultimately provided financial relief and stability.

To prevent future tax issues and enhance their financial well-being, we continued to work with Jake and Linda post-sale.

We developed a more comprehensive financial plan tailored to their retirement needs, focusing on investment in income-producing assets and regular tax planning reviews. This proactive approach aimed to secure their financial future and prevent similar situations from arising.

The case of Jake and Linda is a great example of the effectiveness of asset liquidation as a strategy for managing substantial tax liabilities.

With professional guidance, the retired couple was able to manage the complexities of asset sales and tax implications successfully.

We ensure that every action taken aligns with the broader financial goals and stability of our clients.

The answer to the question posed in the chapter title means dire consequences are looming on your way. And things will only get uglier if unpaid taxes persist.

However, with professional help, you can manage paying your taxes, no matter if you don't have money. In order to resolve your issues, the first step is to get in touch with a professional.

As you can see through the above case studies, we have done it many times, and we can do it for you as well.

Unpaid Taxes + No Money = Consequences

Unpaid Taxes + No Money + ***Us*** = Solutions with Peace of Mind

Chapter 3: Failure-to-File Penalties

I believe we should all pay our taxes with a smile. I tried, but they wanted cash.

(Anonymous)

The **Failure-to-File Penalty** is a penalty imposed on taxpayers who fail to file their required federal tax returns by the deadline, including extensions.

The IRS imposes several penalties related to the failure to file tax returns, which are crucial for taxpayers to understand in order to avoid significant financial consequences.[2]

Broadly speaking, there are a few main categories or types of penalties that can be imposed. These include Penalty for Fraudulent Failure to File, Minimum Penalty for Late Filing, and Combined Penalty Limits. We will be discussing these penalties in more detail in this chapter, along with their specific-case penalties.

But for now, it's important to remember that if you don't file your tax return by the deadline (including extensions), the IRS imposes a failure-to-file penalty. This penalty is generally 5% of the unpaid taxes for each month or part of a month that a tax return is late. The penalty starts accruing the day after the tax-filing due date and can build up to a maximum of 25% of your unpaid taxes. To illustrate this with a real-life scenario, let's consider the case of Emily, an independent graphic designer.

Case Study: Emily's Struggle with the Failure-to-File Penalty

Emily, due to personal and professional distractions, overlooked filing her federal income tax return for the year. She

[2] https://www.irs.gov/payments/penalties

had an estimated tax liability of $4,000 but failed to file her return by the April 15 deadline. Unfortunately, Emily did not realize her oversight until three months later, in mid-July.

Since Emily missed the filing deadline, the Failure-to-File Penalty kicked in the day after the tax deadline, April 16. The penalty for failure to file was 5% of the unpaid taxes for each month or part of a month that the return was late. Here's how Emily's penalties accrued:

Initial Month (April 16 to May 15): The penalty for the first month was 5% of her unpaid tax ($4,000), which equals $200.

Subsequent Months: The same calculation applied for the next two months (until July 15), adding an additional $400 over these two months.

At this point (three months late), Emily's total Failure-to-File Penalty amounted to $600, which was 15% of her original tax due.

If Emily continued to delay her filing, she could accrue this penalty monthly up to a maximum of 25% of her unpaid taxes. In her case, the maximum penalty would be $1,000 if her return remained unfiled beyond five months.

Upon realizing her mistake, Emily quickly sought our assistance. We helped her file her overdue tax return and negotiate with the IRS to minimize further penalties and interest. We also advised her on how to apply for penalty abatement, which reduced some of the penalties as we demonstrated a reasonable cause for her failure to file on time.

Emily filed her return, paid the tax owed plus the accrued penalties, and submitted a request for penalty abatement based on her circumstances. After reviewing her case, the IRS granted a partial abatement, reducing her penalty based on her history of timely filings in previous years and the reasonable cause presented.

Emily was able to mitigate some of the penalties with our help, but the financial impact and stress could have been easily avoided with more timely action. It is essential that all taxpayers keep track of tax deadlines and obligations to avoid unnecessary penalties.

1040 Minimum Penalty for Late Filing

If your return is filed more than 60 days after the due date or extended due date, the minimum penalty is either $435 or 100% of the unpaid tax, whichever is less. This ensures that there is a significant penalty even if the 5% monthly penalty calculated on the unpaid taxes would be lower.[3] Let's examine this through the example involving Tom, a photographer.

Case Study: Tom's Encounter with the Minimum Penalty for Late Filing

Tom, a seasoned photographer, experienced a challenging year with multiple personal issues that distracted him from his usual meticulous tax preparation. His estimated tax liability was $3,000 for the year. Tom's tax return was due on April 15, but he missed this deadline and also neglected to request an extension.

The Minimum Penalty for Late Filing becomes applicable when a return is filed more than 60 days after the due date. For Tom, this penalty came into effect after June 14 (60 days post-April 15).

Since Tom's unpaid tax was $3,000, the penalty was calculated as 100% of the unpaid tax. However, the IRS capped this penalty at $435, making this the amount Tom was liable to pay, which was less than the full unpaid tax amount but significantly higher than typical monthly late penalties.

---

[3] https://turbotax.intuit.com/tax-tips/irs-letters-and-notices/guide-to-irs-tax-penalties-how-to-avoid-or-reduce-them/L7Unetw5B

Tom realized his oversight in mid-July, more than 90 days after the original due date. Upon recognizing his error, he contacted our firm for advice. We helped Tom file his overdue return immediately and explained the implications of the minimum penalty. We also reviewed Tom's case to determine if there was any basis for requesting penalty abatement based on reasonable cause.

Tom filed his late return and paid the tax owed along with the $435 minimum late filing penalty. We also helped him submit a detailed explanation to the IRS, requesting abatement of the penalty due to his previous consistent filing history and the personal hardships he faced during the year. The IRS reviewed his situation and, acknowledging his past compliance and the circumstances, decided to abate the penalty, offering Tom some financial relief.

1040 Penalty for Fraudulent Failure to File

The Penalty for Fraudulent Failure to File is a severe sanction imposed by the IRS when a taxpayer willfully fails to file a tax return with the intent to evade paying taxes.

If the failure to file is found to be fraudulent, the penalty increases. Generally, the IRS charges a much steeper penalty of 15% per month, up to a maximum of 75% of the unpaid taxes.[4]

As you can see, this penalty is significantly harsher than standard failure-to-file penalties, reflecting the seriousness of the intent behind the non-compliance. Let's explore this through a real-life example involving a business owner, Michael.

---

[4] https://www.insightlawfirm.com/irs-matters/penalties-audit-reconsideration-and-other-tax-issues/

Case Study: Michael's Case with Fraudulent Failure to File

Michael owns a thriving electronics store but has increasingly found himself struggling with cash flow issues. In an attempt to alleviate his financial burdens, Michael decided not to file his tax returns for two consecutive years despite substantial business income. His actions were not merely oversight but a deliberate attempt to evade tax responsibilities due to financial pressure, which constituted a fraudulent failure to file.

Michael's tax liability for one year was $20,000; the penalty for the first month alone was 15% of $20,000, which amounted to $3,000. Since his fraudulent behavior continued unaddressed for five months, the penalty was capped at 75% of the unpaid tax, totaling an additional $15,000 on top of the original tax owed.

The IRS initiated an investigation after noticing discrepancies in reported revenues and the lack of filed returns. Upon discovering the intentional omission, Michael was liable for substantial penalties and also faced the potential of criminal charges.

Facing the severity of his situation, Michael sought our help. We negotiated with the IRS to mitigate some of the penalties by arranging for Michael to come into compliance and helped Michael file the overdue tax returns, disclosing all taxable income. We set up a payment plan for both the taxes and the penalties owed.

While Michael was able to avoid prison time, he still faced significant financial repercussions from the penalties and had to adhere strictly to the terms set by the IRS. The resolution of his case involved ongoing monitoring by the IRS to ensure continued compliance.

Taxpayers should be aware that while penalties can be severe, engaging with a tax professional early can provide pathways to resolve outstanding issues and potentially reduce the consequences of such actions.

Combined Penalty Limits

If failure-to-file and failure-to-pay penalties are due in the same month, the total penalty is 5% of the unpaid taxes (4.5% for not filing and 0.5% penalty for not paying). It is calculated monthly or for any part of a month that the return remains unpaid. It is capped at 25%.

If your taxes remain unpaid after five months, the failure-to-file penalty will reach its maximum limit, and the failure-to-pay penalty will accumulate until the taxes are fully paid, which reaches up to 25%.

The combined maximum penalty can amount to 47.5% of the unpaid taxes (22.5% for late filing and 25% for late payment).[5]

Case Study: Helen's Encounter with Combined Penalty Limits

Helen, a freelance graphic designer, found herself in a tight financial situation after an unexpected downturn in job offers. This financial stress led her to both file her federal tax return late and delay her tax payments. She was unaware of the potential penalties that could accumulate from these actions.

Failure-to-pay penalty is 0.5% per month. If both penalties apply in the same month, the IRS combines them, but the total cannot exceed 5% per month.

Helen had a tax due of $10,000:

- The failure-to-file penalty for one month was $500 (5% of $10,000).

[5] https://www.irs.gov/faqs/irs-procedures/collection-procedural-questions/collection-procedural-questions-3

- The failure-to-pay penalty for the same month was $50 (0.5% of $10,000).
- Instead of totaling $550, the combined penalty for any month where both penalties were applicable was capped at $500 (5% of the unpaid taxes).

Upon realizing the severity of her situation, Helen contacted us and explained to us her situation. We helped Helen file her overdue tax return and set up an Installment Agreement to manage her outstanding tax balance.

With our advice, Helen was able to minimize further penalty accruals by quickly coming into compliance. We also guided her through the process of applying for penalty abatement, which the IRS granted based on her previous compliance history and current financial hardships.

By addressing the issues promptly and utilizing our expertise, Helen managed to reduce the overall impact of the penalties. Although she still had to pay a significant amount in penalties and taxes, the damage was less severe than if she had continued to delay.

Helen's situation is a reminder to all taxpayers of the need to maintain timely tax filing and payment practices to avoid compounded penalties and to seek professional help immediately upon realizing that their tax obligations may not be met.

Now that we have an understanding of the main categories of penalties, it's also important to mention that there are certain situation-based or case-based penalties. Let's take a look at those cases below for better understanding.

1120 Failure-to-File Penalty for Income Tax

For corporations, failure to file a corporation income tax return (Form 1120) by the deadline, including extensions, results in a penalty of 5% of the unpaid taxes for each month or part of a month that the return is late, up to a maximum of 25%.[6]

Similar penalties apply to corporations that fail to file their income tax returns (Form 1120) on time.

Case Study: The Impact of Failure-to-File Penalty John Faced Due to Missing His Corporate Income Tax Filing Deadline

John is a software developer who, due to personal distractions and mismanagement of his financial records, missed the April 15 tax filing deadline. Unaware of the severity of penalties associated with late filing, he delayed his tax submission without seeking an extension.

John faced a significant tax liability of $20,000 for the year. As the deadline passed without John filing his return, the IRS began to levy the failure-to-file penalty. As the months progressed, John's penalty began to accrue:

- **First Month:** 5% of $20,000 = $1,000
- **Second Month:** An additional 5%, totaling $2,000 to date
- **Third Month:** The penalty grew to 15% of the unpaid tax = $3,000
- **Six Months:** John's failure-to-file penalty reached the maximum cap of 25% of his unpaid tax = $5,000

At this point, John owed the IRS a total of $25,000, comprising his original tax due plus the maximum failure-to-file penalty.

By mid-October, John realized the seriousness of his situation when he received a notice from the IRS detailing his

---

[6] https://www.irs.gov/instructions/i1120

outstanding tax liability and the penalties imposed. Alarmed by the escalating costs, he came to us to address the situation.

We reviewed John's financial situation and immediately filed the overdue tax return to stop further penalties and also reviewed John's case for possible reasonable cause criteria that might qualify for penalty abatement.

We prepared a detailed explanation and documentation showing that John's failure to file was due to the serious illness of a close family member, which significantly distracted him from his business and tax obligations.

After submitting the request for penalty abatement along with the late tax return, the IRS reviewed John's submission and circumstances. Recognizing the validity of his reasonable cause claim, the IRS granted a reduction in the failure-to-file penalty, cutting it by half to $2,500.

John arranged to pay the remaining $22,500 (including his original tax due and the reduced penalty) through an Installment Agreement, allowing him to manage the payments in a way that was financially feasible without further straining his resources.

With the right support and prompt action, you can rectify your mistakes and mitigate the consequences, even in situations where significant penalties have been assessed.

Form 1120-S (S Corporation)

Penalty Computation

- The penalty for failing to file Form 1120-S by the due date, including extensions, is calculated based on each month or part of a month the return is late.
- The penalty is $220 for each month or part of a month the return is late, multiplied by the number of shareholders the S corporation had during any part of the

corporation's tax year. This penalty can be charged for up to 12 months.[7]

- Maximum Penalty
- The maximum penalty is generally limited to 12 months.
- Reasonable Cause
- If the failure to file on time is due to reasonable cause and not due to willful neglect, the penalty may not be imposed.

Form 1065 (Partnership)

Penalty Computation

- Similar to Form 1120-S, the penalty for failing to file Form 1065 is based on each month or part of a month the return is late.
- The penalty is $220 for each month or part of a month the return is late, multiplied by the number of partners in the partnership during any part of the partnership's tax year. This penalty can also be charged for up to 12 months.

Maximum Penalty

- As with Form 1120-S, the maximum duration for which the penalty can be imposed is 12 months.[8]

Reasonable Cause

- Penalties may not be imposed if the partnership can show that the failure to file on time was due to reasonable cause and not due to willful neglect.

Both penalties emphasize the importance of timely and accurate filing of tax returns for S corporations and partnerships.

---

[7] https://turbotax.intuit.com/tax-tips/small-business-taxes/s-corp-federal-tax-filing-dates/L1U6tYGMt

[8] https://www.investopedia.com/terms/f/form-1065.asp

It's crucial for entities to maintain good compliance practices to avoid these penalties. For more detailed guidance, refer to the Internal Revenue Manual (IRM) sections related to each form and the specific penalty provisions under IRC sections 6698 (for partnerships) and 6699 (for S corporations).

706 & 709: Failure-to-File Penalty for Estate and Gift Taxes

Executors who fail to file an estate tax return (Form 706) by the due date, including extensions, face a penalty of 5% per month, up to a maximum of 25% of the amount due.

Similarly, individuals who fail to file a gift tax return (Form 709) incur a penalty of 5% per month of the tax due, up to a maximum of 25%.[9]

Case Study: Estate Tax Filing Delays for the Estate of Mr. Jonathan Greene

Mr. Jonathan Greene was a prominent real estate investor who passed away, leaving a substantial estate. His will appointed his son, Jake Greene, as the executor. The estate included multiple properties, investments, and valuable personal assets. The total value of the estate easily exceeded the federal estate tax exemption limit, necessitating the filing of an estate tax return (Form 706).

Jake, while grieving the loss of his father, was overwhelmed by the responsibilities of managing the complex estate. Unfamiliar with the intricacies of estate tax law and distracted by the ongoing probate proceedings, he missed the nine-month deadline for filing Form 706.

As a result of not filing the estate tax return on time, the estate faced a failure-to-file penalty. Given that the estate's tax liability

---

[9] https://freemanlaw.com/reasonable-cause-an-estates-defense-against-irss-late-filing-penalties/

was estimated at $500,000, the initial penalty for the first month was $25,000 (5% of $500,000).

Three months post the filing deadline, Jake discovered the oversight after consulting with an estate planning attorney. At this point, the total penalty had accrued to $75,000, which was 15% of the estate's tax liability.

The estate planning attorney quickly assessed the situation and determined that action was needed to mitigate further penalties. Recognizing the need for specialized tax expertise, Jake engaged our firm.

We prepared and filed the overdue Form 706 immediately. Alongside the filing, we also submitted a detailed explanation and a request for penalty abatement. The request outlined Jake's lack of experience with estate matters, the complexity of the estate, and his reliance on certain legal advisors who failed to inform him adequately of the filing requirements.

After reviewing the submission, the IRS recognized the mitigating factors, including Jake's prompt action upon discovering the filing oversight and his good faith effort to comply with tax laws. As a result, the IRS granted a partial abatement of the penalties, reducing the total penalties by 50% to $37,500.

Through professional assistance, Jake was able to substantially reduce the financial burden of penalties on the estate, preserving more of the estate's assets for the beneficiaries.

Case Study: Resolving Gift Tax Filing Delays for Mrs. Elizabeth Carter

Mrs. Elizabeth Carter, a retired school principal, had generously gifted a portion of her investment portfolio to her two grandchildren, intending to support their future education. The value of the gifts exceeded the annual exclusion limit for gift taxes, necessitating the filing of a gift tax return (Form 709).

Elizabeth, unfamiliar with the gift tax filing requirements, missed the April 15 deadline following the year of the gifts.

Due to her oversight, Elizabeth faced significant penalties for not filing the required Form 709 on time.

The total gift tax liability for Elizabeth was calculated to be $10,000, based on the amount by which her gifts exceeded the annual exclusion. Upon missing the filing deadline, the penalty began to accrue:

First Month: 5% of $10,000 = $500

Third Month: 15% of $10,000 = $1,500

Two months after the deadline, Elizabeth was advised by a friend to consult a tax professional regarding her gift tax obligations. Realizing the potential penalties, she promptly contacted us.

We reviewed her situation, confirmed the oversight, and immediately prepared and filed the overdue Form 709 to stop further penalty accrual.

Alongside the filing, we drafted a detailed request for penalty abatement, which included a declaration of her lack of knowledge about gift tax requirements and her immediate action upon becoming aware of her obligations.

Considering Elizabeth's previous clean tax record and the steps taken to rectify the mistake promptly, the IRS granted a reduction in the penalties. The total penalties were reduced by 50% to $750.

Elizabeth was relieved to resolve the issue without the maximum penalties and gained a valuable understanding of gift tax obligations.

990 Failure-to-File Penalty for Non-Profit Organizations

Non-profit organizations must file an annual information return (Form 990). Failing to file for three consecutive years results in automatic revocation of tax-exempt status. Penalties for late filing are $20 per day, with a maximum penalty of the lesser of $10,000 or 5% of the organization's gross receipts for the year.[10]

Case Study: Resolving Form 990 Filing Issues for Green Future Foundation

Green Future Foundation (GFF), a non-profit organization focused on environmental advocacy, experienced significant growth and activity over the past few years.

Amidst the expansion and operational changes, the organization inadvertently neglected to file its annual information return, Form 990, for three consecutive years.

The failure to file Form 990 placed GFF at risk of losing its tax-exempt status, a critical aspect of its operations and fundraising capabilities. Additionally, for each year the form was late, the IRS imposed a daily penalty of $20, with the potential to reach a maximum penalty of $10,000 or 5% of the organization's gross receipts for each year, depending on which was less.

Given that GFF's annual gross receipts averaged around $200,000, the maximum penalty for failing to file Form 990 could reach $10,000 for each of the three years. This situation not only threatened the foundation's financial stability but also its reputation and ability to operate effectively.

---

[10] https://www.nonprofitexpert.com/nonprofit-questions-answers/what-happens-if-my-form-990-is-filed-late/

Upon realization of the oversight during an internal audit, GFF's board members took immediate action by consulting with us.

We conducted a thorough review of GFF's financial activities and previous years' records to prepare the overdue Form 990s and also assessed the situation to determine the best approach to address the non-compliance with the IRS and prevent the revocation of GFF's tax-exempt status.

We expedited the filing of the missing returns and initiated contact with the IRS to explain the non-profit's situation. Alongside the filings, we submitted a detailed request for abatement of penalties and reinstatement of tax-exempt status, citing reasonable cause due to a lack of understanding of the filing requirements by the newly appointed staff and the transition between financial officers during that period.

The IRS reviewed the submissions and acknowledged the non-profit's proactive efforts and transparency in addressing the issue. They accepted the filings, abated the penalties for all three years, and reinstated GFF's tax-exempt status. This resolution allowed GFF to continue its environmental advocacy work without the burden of penalties and with restored tax benefits.

941 & 944 Failure-to-File Penalty for Payroll Taxes

Failure to File Payroll Tax Returns: Businesses are required to file quarterly payroll tax returns (Form 941) or annual form (944) to report wages paid, tips employees received, and taxes withheld. Late filing results in penalties.

Failure to Deposit Payroll Taxes: Employers must deposit employee withholdings (federal income tax and FICA taxes) according to a schedule prescribed by the IRS. Failure to deposit on time results in penalties that can range from 2% to 15% of the underpayment, depending on the lateness of the deposit.[11]

Case Study: Payroll Filing Penalties for Fingertip Technologies

Fingertip Technologies, a mid-sized software development firm, experienced rapid growth over the past year. Amidst the expansion and operational challenges, the company overlooked the importance of timely payroll tax filings. This oversight led to multiple missed deadlines for submitting payroll taxes and associated forms.

Due to missing the quarterly payroll tax filing deadlines, Fingertip Technologies faced substantial penalties. The IRS imposed penalties for late filing of payroll taxes, which included a percentage of the unpaid tax due, along with failure-to-deposit penalties since the payroll taxes were not deposited as required.

For each late month, the IRS assessed a failure-to-file penalty, adding to the financial strain on the company. Fingertip Technologies had a quarterly payroll tax liability of $100,000, so the penalties were calculated as follows:

1. ***Failure-to-File Penalty:*** 5% per month on the unpaid tax, capping at 25%.
2. ***Failure-to-Deposit Penalty:*** Starting at 2% and increasing up to 15%, depending on the lateness of the tax deposit.

By the end of the quarter, the penalties, combined with the original tax due, significantly increased the company's liabilities.

The CFO of Fingertip Technologies recognized the escalating costs associated with non-compliance and immediately sought our help to address the issue.

---

[11] https://www.irs.gov/taxtopics/tc757

As soon as we were on board, we conducted a thorough review of the payroll processes and identified the lapses in tax filing and deposit schedules. The first step taken was to comply immediately with all overdue filings to stop further penalties from accruing.

We negotiated with the IRS, outlining the company's recent growth and the oversight due to transitional operational challenges, and filed for penalty abatement based on reasonable cause, citing the company's previously clean compliance record and the steps taken to rectify the situation once the oversight was recognized.

The IRS decided to reduce the penalties significantly. The failure-to-file penalties were reduced by 50%, and the failure-to-deposit penalties were adjusted based on the shortest delay bracket.

To prevent future occurrences, we helped Fingertip Technologies implement a robust payroll system with automated reminders for filing and deposit deadlines. The company also instituted regular training for its accounting staff on compliance matters to ensure ongoing adherence to tax regulations.

Fingertip Technologies learned a crucial lesson on the importance of payroll compliance, and through proactive measures, they safeguarded their operations against future tax-related challenges.

1099s and W-2s Failure-to-File Penalty for Information Returns

Failure to File Information Returns: This includes forms like 1099s and W-2s, which must be filed to report various types of income other than wages, salaries, and tips. Penalties for failing to file these information returns can range from $50 to $270 per form, depending on how late the forms are filed.[12]

International Reporting Penalties: Failure to file international information returns such as the Report of Foreign Bank and Financial Accounts (FBAR) or Form 8938 (Statement of Specified Foreign Financial Assets) can result in severe penalties, often amounting to the greater of $10,000 or 50% of the account balances per violation.[13]

Case Study: Return Penalties for Pinnacle Consulting Firm

Pinnacle Consulting Firm, a rapidly growing IT consulting company, employed several contractors and freelancers across multiple projects. As the end of the tax year approached, the firm faced the challenge of issuing Form 1099s to its contractors to report their earnings. Due to an oversight in the firm's newly implemented payroll system and a misunderstanding of filing deadlines by the administrative staff, Pinnacle failed to file the required 1099s by the January 31 deadline.

The oversight led to Pinnacle Consulting Firm facing potential penalties for each Form 1099 that was not filed on time. The IRS imposed penalties that ranged from $50 to $270 per form, depending on the duration of the delay. With over 30 contractors engaged throughout the year, the potential penalties impacted the firm's financial health.

Assuming the firm was late by more than 30 days but less than six months, the penalty was $110 per form. For 30 contractors, this would total $3,300.

The financial manager of Pinnacle Consulting Firm, Mr. Alan Smith, came to us for a solution. Alan's primary concern was

---

12 https://www.irs.gov/payments/information-return-penalties
13 https://www.goldinglawyers.com/irs-form-8938-penalty/

to address the overdue filings immediately and minimize the penalties.

We conducted a thorough review of the firm's payroll records to confirm the accuracy of the information required for the 1099s. We expedited the filing of all overdue 1099 forms and communicated with the IRS about the firm's situation.

Alongside the filings, we prepared a detailed explanation for the delay, highlighting the firm's reliance on a new payroll system and the administrative confusion regarding the filing deadlines.

In negotiations with the IRS, we emphasized the firm's good faith efforts to comply as soon as the oversight was identified and the steps taken to prevent future occurrences. We requested a reduction or waiver of penalties based on the firm's otherwise strong compliance history and the corrective actions implemented immediately upon discovery of the non-compliance.

The IRS acknowledged the firm's proactive approach and the role of genuine mistakes in the delay and reduced the penalties by 50%. The total penalties were thus brought down to $1,650, alleviating the financial burden on Pinnacle Consulting Firm. Additionally, the firm implemented a new internal review process to ensure timely and accurate compliance with information return filing requirements in the future.

By taking swift corrective action and demonstrating a commitment to compliance, businesses can significantly reduce the impact of penalties and enhance their operational procedures to prevent similar issues in the future.

Case Study: Managing International Reporting Penalties for Dr. Emma Lawrence

Dr. Emma Lawrence, a medical researcher based in the U.S., worked with several international institutions over the past decade. Due to her extensive collaborations, she maintained bank accounts in Europe and Asia to facilitate financial transactions related to her research.

Unaware of her reporting obligations for these foreign accounts, she neglected to file the Report of Foreign Bank and Financial Accounts (FBAR) and Form 8938 "Statement of Specified Foreign Financial Assets."

Dr. Lawrence's financial oversight came to light during a routine review by her new accountant, who noticed the foreign accounts and immediately recognized the compliance gap. Dr. Lawrence faced potentially severe penalties for not reporting these accounts, which could include fines of $10,000 per account or even 50% of the highest balance in each account if found to be willful neglect.

At the time of discovery, Dr. Lawrence's foreign accounts had aggregate balances exceeding $200,000 at their peak during the reporting period. Non-compliance could, therefore, potentially cost her upward of $100,000 in penalties if the failures were deemed willful.

Realizing the severity of the situation, Dr. Lawrence was proactive in addressing the issue. She consulted us with respect to FBAR and FATCA (Foreign Account Tax Compliance Act) regulations.

We reviewed Dr. Lawrence's case, including her reasons for not filing, which were based on a lack of knowledge rather than an intent to conceal. We prepared and submitted the delinquent FBAR and Form 8938 for the relevant years, along with a detailed letter explaining Dr. Thompson's non-willful misunderstanding of the filing requirements.

We initiated a voluntary disclosure with the IRS before any audit or investigation started, which was crucial in mitigating penalties. We argued for reduced penalties based on reasonable cause and non-willful behavior. The detailed correspondence outlined Dr. Lawrence's extensive international collaboration, her financial transparency in other aspects, and her immediate action upon discovering the filing requirements.

The IRS, considering the voluntary disclosure and the circumstances explained, decided to impose a significantly reduced penalty. Instead of the statutory $10,000 per violation or 50% of the account balances, they imposed a minimal penalty in acknowledgment of her proactive steps and non-willful violation.

The Heightened Scrutiny from the IRS

When taxpayers fail to meet their tax obligations, the IRS may escalate its response beyond initial notices and penalties. The consequences of continued non-compliance can permeate various aspects of a taxpayer's financial life, leading to increased scrutiny and more severe actions.

The heightened scrutiny from the IRS includes more detailed reviews of a taxpayer's past and future submissions and an increased likelihood of being selected for an audit.

Audits involve a thorough examination of the taxpayer's financial records and tax returns to verify accuracy and compliance with tax laws. This process can be time-consuming and stressful, requiring the taxpayer to provide additional documentation and sometimes engage in multiple interactions with the IRS.

For example, consider a small business owner who has repeatedly failed to file returns on time and has accumulated significant tax debt. The IRS may flag this as a pattern of non-compliance, prompting an audit. During this audit, all financial aspects of the business would be closely examined, from income statements to expense receipts, potentially uncovering other areas of non-compliance not initially evident.

The ripple effects of failing to address tax liabilities are extensive. They can lead to invasive IRS actions such as audits and the imposition of liens and levies, all of which carry significant personal and financial consequences. Moreover, the impact on credit scores can hamper both personal and business financial growth for years. As a taxpayer, it's essential for facing such issues to seek resolution proactively, ideally with the assistance of a tax professional who can navigate the complexities of IRS policies and negotiate on your behalf to minimize the adverse effects.

Chapter 4: Accumulation of Interest

Tax penalties imposed on unpaid taxes are already enough to make one's situation worse. But the worst is yet to come…

I don't want to scare you, but a bitter fact is staring us right in the eye—the accumulation of interest on unpaid taxes.

If you fail to pay your federal income taxes on time, the IRS will ultimately impose interest on the outstanding balance as well. Unlike IRS penalties for unpaid or late taxes, interest charges typically cannot be waived or reduced, even if you have a valid reason for the delay, though there are a few exceptions. Also, due to daily compounding, the interest on overdue taxes can accumulate rapidly.[14]

Generally, interest on underpayments begins accruing from the due date of the owed amount and continues until the balance is fully paid.[15]

The exact amount you owe depends on several factors, including whether you filed your tax return on time, the remaining balance, and the current interest rate, among others. The IRS evaluates each late payment individually.

The Calculation of Interest

The IRS interest rate is set by adding 3% to the federal short-term rate. As of March 2024, with the federal short-term annual interest rate at 4.71%, the interest rate on late tax payments was 7.71%.

It's important to remember that interest rates can fluctuate, so this rate may change over time. Interest is calculated daily,

---

[14] https://turbotax.intuit.com/tax-tips/tax-payments/what-are-the-irs-interest-rates-for-late-tax-payments-or-refunds/c9GT7oBcN
[15] https://www.irs.gov/payments/interest

meaning you will owe 0.0082% of the outstanding balance for each day your taxes remain unpaid.[16]

For example, if you owe the IRS $2,000 and are 90 days late with an interest rate of approximately 7%, you can calculate the daily interest charge to be around $0.38. Multiplying this by 90 days results in a total interest charge of $34.20.

Similarly, if you owe the IRS $50,000 and are 90 days late with the same interest rate, the daily interest charge would be about $9.59. Multiplying this by 90 days gives a total interest charge of $863.10.

If the $50,000 debt is 180 days late, the total interest charge would amount to $1,726.20.

I hope you can see how quickly this accumulation of interest can increase the total amount of your tax payments. Again, remember that this interest accrues on a daily basis.

In the long run, you will also be accumulating other troubles for yourself. For example, you will have:

- An **increased debt burden**
- **Prolonged financial strain**
- **Serious impacts on your credit and borrowing options**

It is my sincere advice that you avoid underpayments and late payments to stay away from such a hassle.

Well, I know that life is full of surprises, and troubles come without warning. And I have witnessed it happen time and again as I have helped many of my clients.

That's why I emphasize that you make a practical financial plan as per your financial status and follow it religiously. Scott,

---

[16] https://www.fool.com/investing/how-to-calculate/interest-rate-and-penalties-on-late-taxes/

one of our clients, didn't pay attention to it and landed in hot water big time.

Case Study: Resolving Scott Lane's IRS Debt

Scott is a freelance graphic designer with over a decade of experience in the industry. Despite his success in securing various contracts and projects, Scott faced financial challenges that led to his inability to pay his federal income taxes on time. His financial instability was exacerbated by inconsistent client payments and a lack of a structured financial management system. As a result, Scott had no money to pay the IRS and was 110 days late on his tax payments.

Scott Lane approached us with a significant tax issue. He mentioned that he was unable to pay his IRS debt and had already incurred 110 days of lateness. This situation confirmed accruing interest and potential penalties, creating a compounding financial burden that seemed insurmountable to him.

Scott's unpaid taxes were continuously accruing interest and penalties due to the lateness, significantly increasing the total amount owed. He lacked the funds to make any substantial payments toward his tax debt, further exacerbating his financial strain. The situation was overwhelming for Scott.

To address Scott's tax issues, we implemented a comprehensive approach involving three key strategies. We began by thoroughly assessing his financial situation and tax debt. This included evaluating his income, expenses, and overall financial health.

Based on this assessment, we developed a debt consolidation plan. This strategy aimed to combine his various tax obligations into a manageable single payment structure. By doing so, Scott could more easily track and manage his debt repayment process.

We evaluated Scott's eligibility for OIC to settle their tax debt for less than the full amount owed. After determining that Scott was a suitable candidate, we prepared and submitted the OIC application on his behalf. This process involved providing detailed financial information and a persuasive argument for why the IRS should accept a reduced payment.

Our negotiations with the IRS were successful, resulting in a favorable OIC that significantly reduced Scott's total tax liability. This agreement allowed him to resolve his tax debt with a lump-sum payment that was within his financial means.

To prevent future tax issues, we helped Scott set up an organized system for tracking and paying estimated taxes. This system included introducing budgeting tools to help Scott allocate funds for quarterly estimated tax payments, setting up reminders and alerts to ensure timely payments, and providing ongoing support and consultations to help Scott stay on track with his tax obligations and maintain financial stability.

Through our comprehensive approach, Scott successfully overcame his tax challenges and regained control over his financial situation.

Scott experienced considerable relief from the stress and anxiety associated with his tax debt, knowing that he had a clear path to resolution and ongoing support from our team.

As tax professionals, we can provide effective solutions to you if you are facing significant tax challenges, just like we helped Scott Lane to resolve his IRS debt and achieve long-term financial stability.

Case Study: Resolving Carl Martin's Debt

Carl Martin is an entrepreneur who runs a growing business in the health sector. Despite his success, he faced unexpected business expenses that disrupted his financial stability. This led to his inability to pay taxes on time, resulting in significant interest accumulation and mounting financial pressure.

Mr. Martin approached us with a pressing tax issue. Due to unforeseen business expenses, he failed to pay his taxes, leading to considerable interest accumulation on his outstanding tax debt. This situation created a severe financial strain on his business, threatening its stability and future growth.

Carl's unpaid taxes were continuously accruing interest, significantly increasing the total amount owed. His financial instability was further exacerbated by the challenges of managing cash flow amid unexpected expenses. The complex IRS regulations and the fear of severe penalties added to Carl's stress, necessitating professional intervention to find a viable solution.

To illustrate Carl's problem, let's see the math involved in his tax debt situation:

Initial Tax Debt

- Amount Owed: $50,000
- Interest Rate: 7% annually (0.0192% daily)
- Days Late: 110

Interest Calculation

Daily interest rate:

Daily Interest Rate = 7% / 365 = 0.0192%

Calculate the daily interest charge:

Daily Interest Charge = $50,000 x 0.0192% = $50,000 x 0.000192 = $9.60

Daily Interest Charge = $50,000 x 0.0192% = $50,000 x 0.000192 = $9.60

Calculate the total interest for 110 days:

Total Interest = $9.60 x 110 = $1,056

Total Interest = $9.60 x 110 = $1,056

Total Amount Owed After 110 Days:

Total Amount Owed = $50,000 + $1,056 = $51,056

Total Amount Owed = $50,000 + $1,056 = $51,056

To address Carl's tax issues, we implemented a strategy focusing on three key areas. We began by restructuring his business's finances. This involved a thorough review of his financial statements to identify areas where expenses could be reduced, and cash flow could be improved. We then developed a tailored financial plan that prioritized debt repayment while ensuring the ongoing operational needs of his business were met.

Next, we negotiated a payment plan with the IRS on Carl's behalf. By presenting a detailed financial analysis and demonstrating Carl's commitment to resolving his tax debt, we were able to secure a manageable installment agreement. This plan allowed Carl to make regular, affordable payments toward his tax debt, significantly reducing the immediate financial burden and preventing further interest accumulation.

In addition to restructuring finances and negotiating with the IRS, we advised Carl on effective cash flow management strategies to prevent future tax issues. This included implementing budgeting tools and financial forecasting models to better predict and manage his business's income and expenses.

We also set up a system for timely tax payments, including quarterly estimated tax payments, to ensure Carl remained compliant with IRS requirements.

Through our comprehensive approach, Carl successfully overcame his tax challenges and regained control over his financial situation. The key outcomes included:

- **Financial Restructuring:** Carl's business finances were reorganized to improve cash flow and reduce unnecessary expenses, creating a more sustainable financial structure.

- **Negotiated Payment Plan:** A favorable payment plan with the IRS was secured, allowing Carl to make regular, manageable payments toward his tax debt without jeopardizing his business operations.
- **Improved Cash Flow Management:** Carl implemented effective cash flow management practices, ensuring he could meet his tax obligations on time and avoid future interest and penalties.

Carl experienced significant relief from the stress and anxiety associated with his tax debt. With a clear path to resolution and ongoing professional support, he was able to focus on growing his business without the looming threat of IRS penalties.

We can provide effective solutions to entrepreneurs facing substantial tax challenges, just like we did for Carl.

Case Study: Rachel McDonald

Rachel McDonald inherited an estate but was unaware of the tax responsibilities that came with it. Consequently, she faced significant challenges, including substantial unpaid estate taxes, interest charges on these taxes, and a general lack of awareness about her tax obligations. The estate's financial management was also disorganized, leading to inefficiencies and further complications.

To address Rachel's estate tax issues, first, we conducted a thorough review of the estate's financial situation, identifying areas for improvement and restructuring. This involved analyzing the estate's assets, liabilities, income, and expenses to understand the full scope of its financial health and consolidating all outstanding tax liabilities into a single, manageable account to simplify the payment process.

Next, we negotiated a payment plan with the IRS to address Rachel's unpaid estate taxes. This plan allowed her to pay off the tax debt in manageable installments. We prepared and submitted detailed financial documents to the IRS, demonstrating Rachel's financial situation and her inability to pay the full amount immediately, and engaged in negotiations with the IRS to secure a payment plan that suited Rachel's financial capabilities.

To prevent future tax issues, we provided Rachel with guidance on managing the estate's cash flow more effectively. This included creating a budget that allocated funds for tax payments and other essential expenses, advising on strategies to optimize income from the estate's assets, and implementing a system to monitor and control expenses.

We also addressed the backlog of unpaid taxes and negotiated with the IRS to reduce the accrued interest charges. We presented a case to the IRS that highlighted Rachel's unawareness of her tax obligations and requested a reduction in interest charges based on her circumstances. Additionally, we worked with the IRS to establish a clear and fair resolution for the outstanding tax liabilities.

To ensure long-term financial stability, we streamlined the estate's financial affairs. This involved setting up a systematic record-keeping process to track income, expenses, and tax obligations accurately, implementing regular reviews of the estate's financial status, and providing ongoing tax planning advice to ensure compliance with tax regulations and optimize the estate's financial performance.

By restructuring the estate's finances, negotiating a manageable payment plan, and advising on effective cash flow management, we successfully helped Rachel resolve her tax issues with the IRS. The negotiated payment plan and reduced interest charges significantly alleviated her financial burden, and the streamlined financial management system ensured the estate's long-term stability and compliance with tax obligations.

To arrange immediate funds to start paying her unpaid taxes and manage the estate, we also helped her liquidate a certain part of the estate.

Rachel's case establishes the importance of understanding tax obligations associated with inherited estates and the value of professional assistance in dealing with complex tax issues.

Our comprehensive approach not only resolves your tax problems but also establishes a foundation for better financial management, ensuring all of your assets remain in good standing with the IRS.

If you are dealing with similar issues related to accumulated interest on taxes, we are here to assist you in managing and resolving your tax obligations.

Chapter 5: Liens and Levies

Tax liens and levies are potent mechanisms utilized by the IRS to enforce the collection of overdue taxes.

It is essential to comprehend the ramifications of liens and levies, as they can profoundly impact an individual's financial health and a company's operational capabilities.

Safeguarding personal assets and maintaining business continuity necessitates well-informed strategies and prompt action when addressing liens and levies.

What is a Tax Lien?

A tax lien is a legal claim imposed by the government on the properties of individuals or businesses that fail to settle their tax debts. The IRS uses liens as security for these debts, ensuring the government's legal right to seize property if the debt remains unpaid. This lien extends to all of a taxpayer's assets, including property, securities, and vehicles, and it can also apply to assets acquired while the lien is in effect.

When the IRS determines that taxes are owed and remain unpaid, it may file a Notice of Federal Tax Lien. This notice serves as a public document that alerts creditors that the government has a legal right to a debtor's property. The filing of the notice generally occurs after the IRS has assessed the liability, sent a Notice and Demand for Payment, and found that the tax remains unpaid. The lien attaches to all current and future assets and can significantly impact a debtor's ability to transact using these assets.[17]

---

[17] https://www.investopedia.com/terms/f/federal-tax-lien.asp

Consequences of Tax Liens

The repercussions of a tax lien are wide-ranging and can deeply impact an individual's or business's financial health:

Credit Score Impact: Once a tax lien is filed, it can significantly damage your credit score and make it difficult to obtain new credit, refinance existing loans, or secure favorable credit terms.

Asset Restrictions: You may have difficulty selling or refinancing any of your assets, as the lien needs to be satisfied (paid or arrangements made regarding the debt) before any transaction can be completed.

Business Operations: For businesses, it can harm their ability to acquire financing, which can affect daily operations and the ability to expand. Suppliers and creditors may also be hesitant to extend credit, seeing the business as a higher-risk entity.

Public Record: Since tax liens are a matter of public record, they can tarnish the reputation, potentially leading to lost business opportunities or strained personal and business relationships. [18]

Tax liens serve as an essential tool for the IRS to compel payment of overdue taxes and can lead to significant challenges for those who find themselves under such a burden. Therefore, professional intervention is crucial in addressing and resolving tax liens, helping individuals and businesses settle their tax obligations, and mitigating the adverse effects.

What is a Tax Levy?

A tax levy involves the actual seizure of property to satisfy a tax debt. Unlike a lien, which is a legal claim against property used as security for the tax debt, a levy physically takes possession of

[18] https://www.irs.gov/businesses/small-businesses-self-employed/understanding-a-federal-tax-lien

property to settle the outstanding debt. This can include garnishing wages, taking money from bank accounts, and seizing and selling vehicles, real estate, and other personal property.[19]

The process of a tax levy begins after the IRS has assessed the tax, sent a Notice and Demand for Payment, and found that the taxpayer has neglected or refused to pay the debt. Before a levy is issued, the IRS must also send a Final Notice of Intent to Levy and a Notice of Your Right to A Hearing at least 30 days before the levy is initiated.[20] This notice can be given in person, left at the taxpayer's home or workplace, or sent to the last known address by registered or certified mail. If the taxpayer does not respond or make arrangements to pay their taxes, the IRS can proceed with the levy.

Consequences of Tax Levies

The implications of a tax levy are immediate and severe, often causing significant disruption to an individual's or business's financial and personal life:

Direct Seizure of Funds and Assets: The most direct impact of a tax levy is the seizure of money from bank accounts or the garnishment of wages. For businesses, the IRS can also seize receivables, which can cripple operations that depend on steady cash flow.

Sale of Property: The IRS has the authority to seize and sell valuable property, such as cars, boats, and houses, to cover the unpaid taxes. This not only affects the taxpayer's asset base but also their family life and living conditions.

Long-term Financial Strain: A levy can drain financial resources, leaving little to cover basic living expenses. For

---

[19] https://www.investopedia.com/terms/l/levy.asp
[20] https://www.taxpayeradvocate.irs.gov/notices/notice-of-intent-to-levy/

individuals, this might mean an inability to pay for housing or medical expenses; for businesses, it could result in an inability to pay employees or suppliers.

Reputational Damage: For both individuals and businesses, being subjected to a levy can damage reputations. For businesses, it can signal financial instability to suppliers and customers; for individuals, it can cause personal embarrassment and stress.

Due to the severe and immediate nature of levies, it is crucial for taxpayers facing this threat to seek immediate professional help. Tax professionals can assist in negotiating with the IRS to set up payment plans, offer in compromise, or other alternatives to avoid levy actions. Additionally, understanding your rights and options when facing a levy can help mitigate the negative impacts and potentially avert the seizure of assets.

Case Study: Resolving Tax Lien Issues for Shawn Stewart

Shawn Stewart, a small business owner, was dismayed to discover that his credit score had significantly plummeted due to an IRS lien placed on his property for unpaid business taxes. The lien not only affected his personal credit but also posed a serious challenge for his business, making it difficult to secure financing essential for growth and operations. The impact on his credit score created a ripple effect, hindering his ability to obtain loans, negotiate favorable terms with suppliers, and maintain a healthy cash flow.

Shawn's situation was precarious. The unpaid business taxes had accumulated over time, leading to the IRS taking this severe action. The lien was a public record, visible to creditors and lenders, severely limiting Shawn's financial options. This scenario threatened the sustainability of his business, as he struggled to manage day-to-day operations without the necessary financial backing.

Seeking a way out of this financial quagmire and trying to fix this problem on his own only worsened the problem at that point. Eventually, Shawn reached out to us for professional assistance. Our team promptly assessed his financial situation and the specifics of the IRS lien. We understood that a multifaceted approach was necessary to resolve the immediate issue and prevent future occurrences.

Our first step was to restructure Shawn's business finances. We conducted a thorough analysis of his business's financial health, identifying areas where expenses could be reduced and revenue streams could be optimized. This restructuring aimed to improve his business's overall financial stability and generate the funds needed to address his tax liabilities.

Simultaneously, we entered into negotiations with the IRS on Shawn's behalf. We presented a detailed proposal, emphasizing his willingness to rectify the situation and his commitment to meeting his tax obligations. Our goal was to negotiate a payment plan that was manageable for Shawn while satisfying the IRS's requirements. The payment plan would allow Shawn to pay off his tax debt over time without crippling his business operations.

In addition to negotiating the payment plan, we advised Shawn on effective cash flow management strategies. We worked with him to develop a budget that prioritized tax payments and other critical expenses. This proactive approach was designed to prevent future tax issues and ensure that Shawn could maintain a positive cash flow, which is essential for his business's ongoing operations.

Our negotiation efforts with the IRS were successful. We secured a payment plan that was both realistic for Shawn and acceptable to the IRS. As part of the agreement, the IRS withdrew the lien from his property. This withdrawal was a significant victory, as it immediately improved Shawn's creditworthiness and removed the public record of his tax delinquency.

With the lien withdrawn, Shawn began the process of restoring his credit score. We provided guidance on steps he could take to rebuild his credit, such as making timely payments, reducing existing debt, and monitoring his credit report for inaccuracies. Over time, these efforts helped him improve his credit score, restoring his financial credibility.

Case Study: Resolving IRS Levy Issues for Becky Kingston

Becky Kingston found herself in a dire financial situation when the IRS imposed a levy on her bank accounts due to unpaid tax debt. This levy effectively froze her accounts, leaving her unable to access the funds needed to cover her essential expenses, including rent, utilities, and daily living costs. The sudden restriction on her financial resources created an immediate and severe hardship, disrupting her ability to manage her personal and professional responsibilities.

The IRS levy was a result of accumulating tax liabilities that had reached a critical point. Despite her efforts to address her tax obligations, Becky's financial situation had deteriorated, leading to this drastic action by the IRS. The levy not only immobilized her funds but also threatened to escalate, potentially targeting her wages and other assets.

Recognizing the urgency of Becky's predicament, she sought our professional assistance. Our team quickly assessed her financial situation and the specifics of the IRS levy. We understood that immediate action was necessary to relieve the financial pressure and restore her access to her funds.

Our first step was to appeal the levy on Becky's behalf. We contacted the IRS and presented a detailed case demonstrating the financial hardship the levy was causing. We provided evidence of her essential expenses and the impact the frozen accounts had on her ability to meet those obligations. Our goal was to highlight that the levy was causing undue hardship and to request its immediate release.

In parallel with the appeal, we began negotiations with the IRS to establish an installment agreement for Becky's tax debt. We conducted a thorough analysis of her financial situation, including her income, expenses, and any available assets. Based on this analysis, we proposed an installment agreement that reflected her ability to pay. This agreement would allow Becky to address her tax liabilities over time without jeopardizing her financial stability.

Our prompt action and thorough preparation were crucial in persuading the IRS to consider our appeal. We maintained constant communication with IRS representatives, providing any additional documentation and information they required. Our persistence paid off when the IRS agreed to release the levy on Becky's bank accounts, recognizing the financial hardship it was causing.

The release of the levy was a significant relief for Becky. It restored her access to her bank accounts, allowing her to cover her essential expenses and regain her financial stability. With the immediate crisis resolved, Becky could focus on adhering to the installment agreement we had negotiated, ensuring that her tax debt would be systematically addressed without further disruptions.

In addition to negotiating the installment agreement, we provided Becky with guidance on effective financial management strategies. We helped her develop a budget that prioritized her tax payments and essential expenses, ensuring that she could maintain her financial stability while meeting her obligations to the IRS. We also advised her on strategies to prevent future tax issues, such as setting aside funds for tax payments and maintaining accurate financial records.

Case Study: Resolving an IRS Levy for Joseph's Landscaping Business

Joseph, the owner of a small landscaping business, found himself in a dire financial situation when the IRS placed a levy on his business. The levy, targeting his business bank accounts and receivables, posed a significant threat to his operations. It jeopardized his ability to pay suppliers and employees, putting the survival of his business at risk.

The IRS levy came as a shock to Joseph. Despite his efforts to manage his finances, outstanding tax liabilities had accumulated, leading to this drastic action. The immediate impact was severe; with his business accounts frozen, Joseph faced an urgent cash flow crisis. Without access to his funds, he could not pay his suppliers, who were essential for maintaining inventory and continuing operations. Additionally, his employees, who relied on their wages for their livelihoods, were left in uncertainty.

Recognizing the critical nature of the situation, Joseph sought professional assistance. We stepped in to negotiate with the IRS on his behalf. Understanding the urgency, we moved quickly to assess his financial standing and the extent of his tax liabilities. Our primary goal was to alleviate the immediate pressure on his business while developing a long-term solution to address the outstanding debt.

Our approach involved several key steps. First, we communicated with the IRS to request an immediate release of the levy. We presented a comprehensive proposal highlighting Joseph's commitment to resolving his tax issues and the detrimental impact the levy had on his business. Emphasizing the importance of maintaining operations, we negotiated for a structured payment arrangement that would allow Joseph to pay off his debt over time without crippling his business.

In parallel, we worked to secure a partial lien release. This step was crucial in restoring some level of financial normalcy to Joseph's business. By negotiating a partial release, we aimed to unfreeze a portion of his accounts, enabling him to meet his essential financial obligations, including payroll and supplier payments. This partial relief was a lifeline for Joseph, allowing him to stabilize his business operations.

Throughout the process, we maintained open lines of communication with both Joseph and the IRS. Our goal was to ensure that all parties were aligned and that the negotiated terms were both feasible for Joseph and acceptable to the IRS. This collaborative approach was instrumental in reaching a resolution that addressed the immediate crisis while laying the groundwork for long-term financial recovery.

The intervention proved successful. The IRS agreed to release the levy in exchange for the structured payment arrangement and the partial lien release. This agreement provided Joseph with the breathing room he needed to continue his business operations without the constant threat of financial collapse. With the levy lifted, Joseph was able to access his funds, pay his suppliers, and ensure that his employees received their wages.

Case Study: Resolving an IRS Lien for Scarlet Depp

Scarlet Depp faced a dire situation when the IRS placed a lien on her home due to unpaid personal taxes. The threat of losing her property was a constant source of stress and anxiety, as her home was not only a valuable asset but also a place of personal significance and stability.

Scarlet had fallen behind on her taxes due to unforeseen financial hardships. The accumulating interest and penalties made it increasingly difficult for her to catch up, and the IRS eventually took action by placing a lien on her home. This lien jeopardized her ability to maintain her home and affected her credit rating, further compounding her financial difficulties.

Upon consulting with Scarlet, we understood the critical need to prevent the seizure of her home. As for the first step, we opened a line of communication with the IRS to discuss her case and convey her willingness to resolve the debt. It was essential to demonstrate Scarlet's genuine intention to comply with tax obligations while highlighting her current financial constraints.

We began by gathering detailed information about Scarlet's financial situation, including her income, expenses, and assets. This comprehensive financial profile allowed us to present a clear and accurate picture to the IRS. Our goal was to negotiate a solution that would prevent the seizure of her home and lead to the release of the lien.

Next, we proposed a structured payment plan to the IRS. This plan took into account Scarlet's ability to pay, ensuring the monthly installments were manageable given her financial situation. We emphasized that this arrangement would enable Scarlet to meet her tax obligations without losing her home, thereby preserving her primary residence and financial stability.

Our negotiations focused on leveraging Scarlet's willingness to comply and the realistic constraints of her financial position. We stressed that a reasonable payment plan was in the best interest of both parties, as it would facilitate the recovery of unpaid taxes without resorting to the drastic measure of seizing her home.

After several rounds of discussions, the IRS agreed to our proposed payment plan. This agreement provided immediate relief to Scarlet, as it prevented the imminent threat of losing her home. The lien on her property was released, restoring her peace of mind and allowing her to focus on maintaining her financial health.

Throughout the process, we also provided Scarlet with guidance on financial management and tax compliance to help her avoid similar situations in the future. This included advice on budgeting, tax planning, and maintaining accurate financial records.

Our intervention enabled Scarlet to negotiate with the IRS successfully. By leveraging her willingness to comply and presenting a clear financial picture, we established a manageable payment plan that prevented the seizure of her home and led to the release of the lien.

Case Study: Facilitating Property Refinancing for Riley Westward by Resolving a Tax Lien

Riley Westward, a homeowner looking to refinance his property to benefit from lower interest rates, encountered a significant obstacle when he discovered an existing tax lien on his home. The lien, a legal claim against the property due to unpaid taxes, made it impossible for Riley to proceed with the refinancing. This situation not only delayed his plans but also threatened his financial goals.

The tax lien had been placed by the IRS due to outstanding tax liabilities. While Riley was aware of his tax debt, he had not anticipated the profound impact it would have on his ability to manage his finances and take advantage of favorable market conditions. The lien had to be satisfied before any refinancing transaction could move forward, presenting a daunting challenge.

Recognizing the urgency of Riley's predicament, he sought our professional assistance. Our team quickly assessed the situation, understanding that time was of the essence to capitalize on the lower interest rates available. We developed a strategic plan to address the tax lien efficiently, ensuring Riley could proceed with his refinancing as soon as possible.

Our first step was to verify the details of the tax lien and Riley's outstanding tax debt. We reviewed his financial records and communicated directly with the IRS to obtain a clear understanding of the amounts owed and the requirements for lifting the lien. With this information in hand, we outlined a plan to expedite the payment of Riley's tax debt.

We advised Riley on the most effective way to secure the necessary funds to pay off his tax liabilities. Given his urgency to refinance, we explored various options, including short-term loans and liquidation of certain assets, to quickly gather the required amount. Riley chose a method that was both feasible and aligned with his financial situation, ensuring he could meet the IRS's demands promptly.

Once the funds were secured, we facilitated the payment process, ensuring that all transactions were accurately documented and swiftly processed. We then submitted a formal request to the IRS for a certificate of discharge for the lien. This certificate would formally remove the lien from Riley's property records, clearing the way for his refinancing application to proceed.

Throughout the process, we maintained constant communication with the IRS to ensure there were no delays or misunderstandings. Our team's experience and knowledge of IRS procedures were instrumental in navigating the complexities of obtaining a lien discharge. We provided the IRS with all necessary documentation and followed up diligently to expedite the issuance of the certificate.

The result was a successful and timely resolution. Riley received the certificate of discharge, effectively removing the tax lien from his property. This pivotal step allowed him to move forward with the refinancing process, securing a new mortgage with a lower interest rate. The refinancing not only reduced his monthly payments but also provided him with additional financial flexibility and stability.

If you are facing challenges with IRS liens and levies, our team is dedicated to assisting you through every step of the process, from appealing levies and negotiating installment agreements to providing strategic financial guidance.

We understand the urgency and sensitivity of these matters and are committed to helping you achieve a resolution that restores your financial stability. Don't hesitate to reach out for professional assistance in managing and resolving your tax obligations effectively.

In each case study, you can see the importance of having an expert was better than going alone. Whether dealing with complex tax issues, navigating legal challenges, or managing financial transactions, the expertise and experience of a professional can make a significant difference in the outcome. Experts bring specialized knowledge, reduce risks, and provide valuable insights that can help avoid costly mistakes and ensure compliance with regulations.

Chapter 6: Tax Refund Opportunities

Tax refund opportunities refer to the various ways taxpayers can reduce their taxable income or directly reduce their tax liability, resulting in a refund from the government. These opportunities include tax deductions, tax credits, and other adjustments that lower the amount of income subject to tax or decrease the overall tax owed.[21]

Accurate tax filing is crucial to ensure you can claim all eligible tax refunds since the tax code is complex and filled with numerous opportunities for deductions and credits that can significantly impact your refund. Filing accurately means meticulously recording income, expenses, and eligible deductions and credits, ensuring that nothing is missed.

Common Mistakes That Lead to Missed Tax Refunds

Several common mistakes can lead to missed refunds. Being aware of these pitfalls can help ensure that you claim all the refunds you are entitled to. Several mistakes are commonly made that may cause taxpayers to miss out on refunds they are entitled to claim. Awareness of these pitfalls can help ensure you receive all eligible refunds.

Many taxpayers miss out on tax refunds simply because they are unaware of them. Common examples include education credits, energy-efficient home improvement credits, and medical expense deductions. Many taxpayers overlook potential tax refunds simply because they are unaware of them. Examples include credits for education, energy-efficient home improvements, and deductions for medical expenses.

---

[21] https://www.investopedia.com/terms/t/tax-refund.asp

Incomplete or incorrect documentation can lead to missed deductions. So, you must ensure to keep thorough records of all deductible expenses and ensure that they are correctly reported. Incomplete or inaccurate documentation can lead to missed deductions. Therefore, it is crucial to maintain detailed records of all deductible expenses and ensure they are accurately reported.

Choosing the incorrect filing status can result in a less favorable tax refund outcome. For instance, single parents might benefit more from filing as head of household rather than single. Selecting the wrong filing status can lead to a less favorable refund outcome. For example, single parents might benefit more from filing as head of household rather than as single.

Failing to report all sources of income or misreporting income can not only lead to penalties but also affect the amount of refund due. Failure to report all sources of income or incorrect reporting of income can result not only in penalties but also in a reduction of the refund amount owed.

Some taxpayers opt for the standard deduction without considering whether itemizing deductions might result in a higher refund. It's essential to compare both options to see which one offers the most benefit. Some taxpayers choose the standard deduction without considering whether itemizing deductions could result in a larger refund. It is important to compare both options to determine which offers the greatest benefit.

Tax Deductions

Tax deductions reduce the amount of income that is subject to tax, effectively lowering your taxable income. By claiming these deductions, you can decrease the portion of your income that is taxed, resulting in potential tax savings.[22] Here are some common examples:

---

[22] https://taxfoundation.org/taxedu/glossary/tax-deduction/

Homeowners can deduct the interest paid on their mortgage, which can significantly reduce taxable income.

If your medical expenses exceed a certain percentage of your adjusted gross income (AGI), you can deduct those costs. This includes expenses for medical care, prescriptions, and medical equipment.

Donations made to qualifying charitable organizations can be deducted from your taxable income.

Known as the SALT deduction, taxpayers can deduct state and local income, sales, and property taxes up to a certain limit.

Interest paid on student loans can be deducted, providing relief for those repaying educational debts.[23]

You must maintain detailed records of your expenses to substantiate your deductions in case of an audit. This includes keeping receipts, invoices, and bank statements that reflect the deductions claimed. Proper documentation ensures that you can confidently claim all eligible deductions without fear of rejection or penalties from the IRS. If you find it overwhelming, don't hesitate to get in contact with a professional. Tax deductions reduce the amount of income that is subject to tax, effectively lowering your taxable income. By claiming these deductions, you can decrease the portion of your income that is taxed, resulting in potential tax savings. Here are some common examples:

- Homeowners can deduct the interest paid on their mortgage, which can significantly reduce taxable income.
- If your medical expenses exceed a certain percentage of your adjusted gross income (AGI), you can deduct those

---

[23] https://turbotax.intuit.com/tax-tips/tax-deductions-and-credits/10-popular-tax-deductions/L9JesBWTQ

costs. This includes expenses for medical care, prescriptions, and medical equipment.

- Donations made to qualifying charitable organizations can be deducted from your taxable income.
- Known as the SALT deduction, taxpayers can deduct state and local income, sales, and property taxes up to a certain limit.
- Interest paid on student loans can be deducted, providing relief for those repaying educational debts.

You must maintain detailed records of your expenses to substantiate your deductions in case of an audit. This includes keeping receipts, invoices, and bank statements that reflect the deductions claimed. Proper documentation ensures that you can confidently claim all eligible deductions without fear of rejection or penalties from the IRS. If you find it overwhelming, don't hesitate to contact a professional.

Tax Credits

Tax credits directly reduce the amount of tax you owe, making them even more valuable than deductions. They are subtracted from your tax liability on a dollar-for-dollar basis. Here are some examples:

Earned Income Tax Credit (EITC) is designed to benefit low to moderate-income working individuals and families. The amount of the credit depends on your income and the number of qualifying children.

Families with qualifying children under the age of 17 can claim **Child Tax Credit**, which directly reduces their tax liability.

American Opportunity Tax Credit helps offset the cost of higher education expenses, covering tuition, fees, and course materials for the first four years of post-secondary education.24 Tax credits directly reduce the amount of tax you owe, making them even more valuable than deductions. They are subtracted from your tax liability on a dollar-for-dollar basis. Here are some examples:

- The Earned Income Tax Credit (EITC) is designed to benefit low to moderate-income working individuals and families. The amount of the credit depends on your income and the number of qualifying children.
- Families with qualifying children under the age of 17 can claim the Child Tax Credit, which directly reduces their tax liability.
- The American Opportunity Tax Credit helps offset the cost of higher education expenses, covering tuition, fees, and course materials for the first four years of post-secondary education."

Distinction Between Refundable and Non-Refundable Credits

Refundable credits can reduce your tax liability to below zero, resulting in a refund. For example, if you owe $500 in taxes and qualify for a $1,000 refundable credit, you would receive a $500 refund.

Non-refundable credits can reduce your tax liability to zero but cannot result in a refund. If you owe $500 in taxes and qualify for a $1,000 non-refundable credit, your tax liability would be reduced to zero, but you would not receive a refund for the remaining $500. Refundable credits can reduce your tax liability to below zero, resulting in a refund. For example, if you owe $500

[24] https://www.irs.gov/newsroom/tax-credits-for-individuals-what-they-mean-and-how-they-can-help-refunds

in taxes and qualify for a $1,000 refundable credit, you would receive a $500 refund.

Non-refundable credits can reduce your tax liability to zero but cannot result in a refund. For instance, if you owe $500 in taxes and qualify for a $1,000 non-refundable credit, your tax liability would be reduced to zero, but you would not receive a refund for the remaining $50

Commonly Missed Opportunities

Education Credits: Many taxpayers overlook credits like the Lifetime Learning Credit, which can help cover tuition and related expenses for higher education.

Energy-Efficient Home Improvements: Credits are available for homeowners who make energy-efficient upgrades to their homes, such as installing solar panels, energy-efficient windows, or heating and cooling systems.

Retirement Savings Contributions Credit: Also known as the Saver's Credit, this is available to low and moderate-income individuals who contribute to a retirement plan, such as an IRA or 401(k).

Maximizing Your Refund

To maximize your tax refund, it's essential to employ effective strategies that ensure you capture all potential refunds. Here are some key strategies:

Start preparing your taxes early to avoid last-minute rushes that can lead to mistakes. Early filing can also expedite your refund process.

Keep detailed records of all income sources, expenses, and receipts throughout the year.

Make a comprehensive list of all possible deductions and credits you might qualify for.

Contribute to retirement accounts like IRAs and 401(k)s, which can reduce your taxable income. Consider Health Savings Accounts (HSAs) if you have a high-deductible health plan, as contributions are tax-deductible.

Ensure you claim all eligible dependents, which can provide significant tax benefits and credits.

Compare the standard deduction with itemized deductions to determine which offers a greater benefit. If itemizing, ensure you accurately calculate and include all deductible expenses. To maximize your tax refund, it's essential to use effective strategies to capture all potential refunds. Here are some key strategies:

- Start preparing your taxes early to avoid last-minute rushes that can lead to mistakes. Early filing can also expedite your refund process.
- Keep detailed records of all income sources, expenses, and receipts throughout the year.
- Make a comprehensive list of all possible deductions and credits you might qualify for.
- Contribute to retirement accounts like IRAs and 401(k)s, which can reduce your taxable income. Consider Health Savings Accounts (HSAs) if you have a high-deductible health plan, as contributions are tax-deductible.
- Ensure you claim all eligible dependents, which can provide significant tax benefits and credits.
- Compare the standard deduction with itemized deductions to determine which offers a greater benefit. If itemizing, ensure you accurately calculate and include all deductible expenses.[25]

[25] https://www.hrblock.com.au/tax-academy/10-tips-to-minimise-your-tax-return

Benefits of Consulting Tax Professionals

Tax professionals have the expertise to deal with complex tax laws, ensure accurate filing, and streamline the tax preparation process, saving you time and effort.

They can uncover deductions and credits you might not be aware of and provide you with tailored advice based on your specific financial situation. They offer support and representation in case of an audit and stay updated on tax law changes, ensuring your returns are compliant and optimized.

How We Helped Maximize Tax Refunds

We have helped people maximize their tax refunds by taking a proactive and thorough approach to their tax preparation, ensuring they captured all potential refunds.

Case Study: Maximizing Tax Refunds for Lisa Jenkins

Lisa Jenkins, an illustration designer, consistently received smaller tax refunds than expected. She was unaware of several industry-specific deductions that could significantly reduce her taxable income and increase her refunds. She had an idea about tax refunds, but it was tough for her how she could maximize the overall refunds.

When we reviewed her past returns, we identified several missed deductions, which included the following:

Lisa worked from a dedicated space in her home but had not claimed the home office deduction. We calculated that 15% of her home was used exclusively for business, leading to a deductible amount of $2,400 per year for utilities and rent.

Lisa had invested $5,000 in high-end computer equipment and software essential for her work. Using the Modified

Accelerated Cost Recovery System (MACRS), we depreciated her equipment over five years, allowing her to deduct $1,000 per year.

Lisa had overlooked several deductible expenses, that included:

- Internet Costs: $600 per year
- Professional Memberships: $300 per year
- Client-Related Travel: $1,200 per year

By filing amended returns for the past three years, we were able to secure significant additional refunds for Lisa. Specifically, the figures for the deductions were as follows:

- Home Office Expenses: $2,400 per year x 3 years = $7,200
- Equipment Depreciation: $1,000 per year x 3 years = $3,000
- Internet Costs: $600 per year x 3 years = $1,800
- Professional Memberships: $300 per year x 3 years = $900
- Client-Related Travel: $1,200 per year x 3 years = $3,600

Total Missed Deductions Identified: $7,200 + $3,000 + $1,800 + $900 + $3,600 = $16,500

Filing the amended returns for these missed deductions resulted in a total additional refund of $16,500 for Lisa. This equated to approximately $5,500 per year. Not only did this secure Lisa a substantial amount in refunds, but it also provided her with crucial knowledge to optimize her tax filings in the future.

By educating Lisa on maintaining detailed records of her business expenses and staying informed about industry-specific deductions, she is now better equipped to maximize her tax savings annually.

Case Study: Reclaiming Substantial Refunds for Randy Smith

Randy Smith, a sales manager in the retail industry, had procrastinated filing his taxes for several years. As a result, he was on the verge of losing a substantial refund due to the statute of limitations for claiming tax refunds, which is typically three years from the original filing deadline. Randy's hesitation to file his overdue returns was primarily due to the complexity of the process and the fear of potential penalties.

Upon understanding Randy's situation, we took the following steps to ensure he reclaimed his refunds:

We conducted a thorough assessment of Randy's financial situation, collecting all necessary documents, including W-2s, 1099s, and receipts for deductible expenses for the past several years.

We identified that Randy had not filed his tax returns for the past three years, and the deadline for claiming refunds for the earliest year was rapidly approaching.

Our team meticulously reviewed Randy's financial records to identify all possible deductions and credits. This included mortgage interest, state and local taxes, charitable contributions, and unreimbursed business expenses.

We prepared the tax returns for the past three years, ensuring accuracy and completeness to maximize his potential refunds.

We prioritized filing the return for the earliest year to ensure that the refund was claimed before the deadline.

We then promptly filed the remaining overdue returns, submitting all required documents to the IRS.

By filing his overdue returns just before the deadline, we successfully reclaimed a substantial refund for Randy. The figures for the refunds were as follows:

Randy Smith, a sales manager in the retail industry, had procrastinated filing his taxes for several years. As a result, he was on the verge of losing a substantial refund due to the statute of limitations for claiming tax refunds, which is typically three years from the original filing deadline. Randy's hesitation to file his overdue returns was primarily due to the complexity of the process and the fear of potential penalties.

Steps Taken to Reclaim Refunds

1. We conducted a thorough assessment of Randy's financial situation, collecting all necessary documents, including W-2s, 1099s, and receipts for deductible expenses for the past several years.
2. We identified that Randy had not filed his tax returns for the past three years, and the deadline for claiming refunds for the earliest year was rapidly approaching.
3. Our team meticulously reviewed Randy's financial records to identify all possible deductions and credits. This included mortgage interest, state and local taxes, charitable contributions, and unreimbursed business expenses.
4. We prepared the tax returns for the past three years, ensuring accuracy and completeness to maximize his potential refunds.
5. We prioritized filing the return for the earliest year to ensure that the refund was claimed before the deadline.
6. We then promptly filed the remaining overdue returns, submitting all required documents to the IRS.

Outcome

By filing his overdue returns just before the deadline, we successfully reclaimed a substantial refund for Randy. The figures for the refunds were as follows:

1. **Tax Year 1:**
2. Total Refund: $3,500
3. Deductions and Credits Applied: Mortgage interest, state and local taxes, charitable contributions.
4. **Tax Year 2:**
5. Total Refund: $4,200
6. Deductions and Credits Applied: Mortgage interest, unreimbursed business expenses, charitable contributions.
7. **Tax Year 3:**
8. **Total Refund:** $3,800
9. **Deductions and Credits Applied:** State and local taxes, mortgage interest, charitable contributions.

Total Refund Reclaimed: $3,500 + $4,200 + $3,800 = $11,500

In addition to securing a total refund of $11,500 for Randy, we provided him with the following benefits:

By filing the returns before the deadline, Randy avoided potential penalties and interest that could have accrued had he continued to delay filing.

We educated Randy on the importance of timely tax filing and maintaining accurate records. We also provided him with strategies to stay organized and proactive in managing his taxes.

We offered Randy ongoing support and assistance for future tax filings, ensuring he remains compliant and maximizes his tax savings.

Case Study: Resolving Delayed Refund for Lidia Depp

Lidia Depp, a marketing manager in the technology sector, experienced significant delays in receiving her tax refund. Upon investigation, it was discovered that errors in her tax return had caused the IRS to flag her submission for review. These errors not only delayed her refund but also caused confusion and frustration for Lidia, who relied on the timely receipt of her refund for financial planning.

To resolve Lidia's issue, we implemented a comprehensive approach involving thorough review, correction of errors, and effective communication with the IRS.

We conducted an initial consultation with Lidia to understand the specifics of her situation and gather all necessary documentation, including her original tax return, W-2s, 1099s, and other relevant financial records.

Our assessment revealed discrepancies in reported income, misclassified deductions, and missing information that had led to the IRS flagging her return.

We meticulously reviewed Lidia's tax return to identify all errors and discrepancies and corrected the inaccuracies, including:

- Ensuring all income was accurately reported and matched the provided W-2s and 1099s.
- Correcting any misclassified deductions and ensuring all eligible credits were claimed accurately.
- Adding any missing information required by the IRS to process the return.

We proactively contacted the IRS to explain the errors and submit the corrected return, provided detailed documentation to support the corrections, and requested expedited processing of Lidia's refund.

Throughout the process, we maintained regular communication with the IRS to monitor the status of Lidia's refund and address any additional questions or concerns they had.

By identifying and correcting the discrepancies in Lidia's tax return, we were able to resolve the delay and expedite the processing of her refund. The specific results were as follows:

Corrected Refund Amount

- Original Expected Refund: $4,500
- Corrected Refund Amount: $5,200

Timely Resolution

- Original Delay Duration: 8 weeks
- Expedited Processing Time After Correction: 3 weeks

Total Additional Refund Secured: $700

Case Study: Resolving Audit Discrepancies for Sammy Rhodes

Sammy Rhodes, an independent contractor in the construction industry, faced an unexpected audit due to discrepancies in his reported income. The IRS flagged his tax return, which resulted in his expected refund being frozen pending the audit's outcome. Sammy was not only concerned about the potential financial impact but also the stress and uncertainty of facing the audit process.

To assist Sammy, we implemented a comprehensive strategy that included representation during the audit, thorough review and resolution of discrepancies, and negotiation with the IRS to release his refund. Here's a detailed breakdown of the steps we took:

We conducted an initial consultation with Sammy to understand his situation and gather all relevant documents, including his tax returns, 1099 forms, and records of income and expenses. Our assessment identified several discrepancies in the reported income and deductions, which triggered the audit.

We represented Sammy during the audit, acting as his advocate and point of contact with the IRS. This included attending all audit meetings and handling communications on his behalf. We prepared a comprehensive response to the IRS's inquiries, supported by detailed documentation and explanations for the discrepancies.

We reviewed Sammy's financial records to identify and correct the discrepancies in his reported income. Common issues addressed included:

- **Unreported Income:** Ensuring all income was accurately reported and matched the 1099 forms provided by his clients.
- **Misclassified Deductions:** Correcting any misclassified or unsupported deductions and ensuring they were accurately documented.
- **Documentation Gaps:** Filling in any gaps in documentation with additional records and receipts to support Sammy's claims.

After resolving the discrepancies, we negotiated with the IRS to release Sammy's frozen refund. We provided a detailed report of our findings and corrections, demonstrating that Sammy's return was now accurate and compliant with tax regulations.

Our efforts resulted in a successful resolution of Sammy's audit and the release of his expected refund. The specific results were as follows:

Corrected Refund Amount

- Original Expected Refund: $6,000
- Adjusted Refund After Audit Resolution: $5,800

Audit Resolution Timeline

- Initial Audit Notification: 12 weeks prior
- Audit Resolution and Refund Release: 6 weeks after our intervention

Total Refund Secured: $5,800

If you are facing challenges with tax refund opportunities, our team is here to support you every step of the way, offering strategic guidance tailored to your needs. We are committed to helping you manage these issues and achieve a resolution that restores your financial stability. Don't hesitate to seek professional assistance to manage and resolve your tax matters effectively.

As illustrated in each case study, having an expert by your side is far more advantageous than tackling these issues alone. Whether dealing with complex tax matters, legal challenges, or financial management, the expertise and experience of a professional can significantly impact the outcome.

As tax experts, we provide specialized knowledge, minimize risks, and offer valuable insights that help avoid costly mistakes and ensure compliance with regulations.

Chapter 7: Loan & Mortgage Applications

Tax returns are a cornerstone of the financial ecosystem, serving as a detailed record of an individual's or business's income, expenses, and other pertinent financial information over a specific period. The importance of tax returns extends beyond merely fulfilling a legal obligation; they provide a transparent and verifiable account of financial activities that are crucial for various financial processes.

Tax returns serve as a primary document for verifying income, which is essential for numerous financial transactions, including applying for loans, securing investments, and even determining eligibility for certain government benefits.[26]

Simply put, tax returns encapsulate the financial behavior and stability of an individual or business, offering a snapshot of economic health that can be used by financial institutions, investors, and government agencies alike.

Connection Between Tax Returns and Loan Approval

When applying for a loan, whether for personal, business, or mortgage purposes, lenders seek to mitigate risk by thoroughly assessing the borrower's financial health. At this point, tax returns play a pivotal role in this assessment. They provide lenders with a verified history of income, which is essential in determining the borrower's ability to repay the loan.[27] This verification is particularly crucial in instances where the borrower's income is

---

[26] https://www.investopedia.com/articles/personal-finance/121614/importance-filing-your-tax-return.asp
[27] https://www.bankrate.com/finance/taxes/tax-return-requirements-for-mortgages-and-loans/

not straightforward, such as for self-employed individuals or those with variable income sources.

Moreover, tax returns help lenders calculate key financial metrics such as the debt-to-income ratio (DTI), which is a critical factor in loan approval decisions.[28]

A lower DTI ratio, as evidenced by consistent and sufficient income reported on tax returns, often leads to more favorable loan terms. Conversely, inconsistencies or discrepancies in tax returns can raise red flags, leading to delays, additional scrutiny, or even denial of the loan application.[29]

These connections underline the indispensable role that tax returns play in the loan approval process, serving as a tool for both verification and financial assessment that ultimately influences a lender's decision.

Verification of Income

One of the primary reasons lenders request tax returns during the loan application process is to verify the applicant's reported income. Tax returns provide a detailed and accurate history of income over a specific period, usually the last two years. This verification process is essential to ensure that the income reported on the loan application is accurate and consistent with official records.[30] This way, lenders can verify that the applicant has a stable and reliable source of income, which is crucial for determining their ability to repay the loan.

---

[28] https://www.consumerfinance.gov/ask-cfpb/what-is-a-debt-to-income-ratio-en-1791/

[29] https://www.thebalance.com/why-lenders-require-tax-returns-1798859

[30] https://www.investopedia.com/ask/answers/042015/why-do-lenders-require-tax-returns.asp

Assessment of Financial Stability

Lenders also use tax returns to assess the financial stability of a loan applicant. Consistent income over several years, as reflected in tax returns, indicates financial stability and reliability, which are key factors in the lender's decision-making process. A steady income stream, particularly from a single source such as employment or a well-established business, reduces the risk for lenders and increases the likelihood of loan approval.[31]

On the other hand, fluctuating income or a sudden drop in earnings might signal financial instability, prompting lenders to take a closer look or even reconsider the loan application.

Debt-to-Income Ratio

The DTI is a critical factor in the loan approval process, and tax returns play a significant role in its calculation. The DTI ratio is the percentage of an applicant's gross monthly income that goes toward paying debts. Lenders use this ratio to determine an applicant's ability to manage monthly payments and repay the loan.[32] Tax returns provide the necessary income information to accurately calculate this ratio. A lower DTI ratio indicates that the borrower has a good balance between debt and income, making them a more favorable candidate for a loan.

Self-Employed and Independent Contractors

Unlike salaried employees who can provide pay stubs as proof of income, self-employed individuals must rely on their tax returns to demonstrate their earnings. Lenders typically require at least two years of tax returns to assess the stability and reliability

---

[31] https://www.thebalance.com/why-lenders-require-tax-returns-1798859

[32] https://www.consumerfinance.gov/ask-cfpb/what-is-a-debt-to-income-ratio-en-1791/

of income from self-employment.[33] This documentation provides a comprehensive view of their business income, expenses, and net profits, which are essential for evaluating their ability to repay the loan.

Red Flags

Inconsistencies or discrepancies are major red flags for lenders and can significantly delay or even prevent loan approval. Common issues include discrepancies between the income reported on tax returns and the income stated on the loan application, large fluctuations in income, or unreported income. These inconsistencies can raise doubts about the applicant's financial stability and honesty, leading lenders to request additional documentation or clarification.[34] In some cases, these red flags might result in the outright denial of the loan application, particularly if the inconsistencies cannot be adequately explained.

Mortgage Loans

Mortgage lenders typically require two to three years of tax returns to evaluate a consistent income stream and ensure that the applicant's reported earnings are accurate.[35] This is particularly important for self-employed borrowers, whose income may vary year by year.

Lenders use tax returns to verify income and cross-check it with other financial documents like W-2s, 1099s, and bank statements. They also look at deductions and other tax-related

---

[33] https://www.investopedia.com/articles/mortgages-real-estate/08/self-employed-mortgage.asp

[34] https://www.bankrate.com/finance/taxes/when-mortgage-lenders-want-more-tax-documents/

[35] https://www.bankrate.com/mortgages/tax-returns-and-mortgages/

information to ensure that the borrower's financial situation is stable enough to manage mortgage payments.[36]

Business Loans

Lenders require several years of both personal and business tax returns to assess the viability of the business and the financial health of its owner.[37] These documents allow lenders to verify revenue, profits, and the overall financial stability of the business.

For small businesses, tax returns are often used to calculate cash flow and the DTI ratios, which are key indicators of the business's ability to repay the loan. Lenders also examine business expenses, deductions, and any potential red flags, such as losses or irregularities in income. A strong financial history reflected in tax returns can significantly improve the chances of securing business financing, while inconsistencies or weak financial performance may lead to denial or less favorable loan terms.[38]

Personal Loans

All lenders may not require tax returns for personal loans, but many do, especially if the borrower is self-employed or has multiple sources of income.[39]

In addition to income verification, lenders may also use tax returns to evaluate an applicant's financial stability by examining deductions, credits, and other financial activities. This helps them assess the risk associated with lending to the applicant.

---

[36] https://www.investopedia.com/articles/pf/12/how-to-get-mortgage-when-self-employed.asp

[37] https://www.forbes.com/advisor/business-loans/business-loan-requirements/

[38] https://www.sba.gov/funding-programs/loans/lender-match

[39] https://www.experian.com/blogs/ask-experian/why-do-lenders-ask-for-tax-returns/

Accuracy and Honesty

One of the most critical best practices for loan applicants is to ensure that their tax returns are filed accurately and honestly. Lenders rely heavily on tax returns to assess an applicant's financial stability and ability to repay the loan. Any discrepancies or inaccuracies can lead to serious consequences, including delays in the loan approval process or even outright denial.

Accurate tax returns provide a true reflection of an applicant's income, expenses, and overall financial situation. Misreporting income or claiming deductions that cannot be substantiated can raise red flags for lenders, leading to additional scrutiny and possible legal consequences. Honesty in tax filings not only helps in the loan approval process but also maintains the applicant's credibility with financial institutions.[40]

Keeping Records

Maintaining thorough and organized records is another essential best practice for applicants seeking loans. Accurate and complete records of income, expenses, and other financial activities make it easier to prepare tax returns and provide supporting documentation during the loan application process.[41]

Good record-keeping ensures that all financial information is readily available and can be verified by lenders. This includes keeping copies of tax returns, receipts, invoices, bank statements, and other financial documents for several years. Properly maintained records not only facilitate the loan application process but also help in managing finances more effectively and ensuring compliance with tax laws.

---

[40] https://www.irs.gov/businesses/small-businesses-self-employed/filing-and-paying-your-business-taxes

[41] https://www.sba.gov/business-guide/manage-your-business/keep-your-business-finances-records-organized

Working with Professionals

Consulting with tax professionals is highly recommended for individuals and businesses preparing for loan applications. These professionals can provide valuable guidance on how to accurately file tax returns, maximize legitimate deductions, and present financial information in a way that enhances the likelihood of loan approval.[42]

They have the expertise to deal with complex tax laws and ensure that tax returns are accurate and compliant with regulations. They help applicants understand their financial situation, plan for the future, and make informed decisions about loans and other financial matters. Working with professionals not only reduces the risk of errors but also provides peace of mind, knowing that the financial information presented to lenders is accurate and well-prepared.[43]

Case Study: Small Business Loan for Expansion

George Miller, the owner of a popular local café in a bustling downtown area, had built his business from the ground up over the past eight years. His café had become a community favorite, known for its cozy atmosphere and artisanal coffee. With a steady stream of loyal customers, John saw an opportunity to expand his business by opening a second location. To finance this expansion, George needed a small business loan that would cover the costs of leasing a new space, purchasing additional equipment, and hiring more staff.

George approached a lender with his loan application, confident that his café's success and strong customer base would

---

[42] https://www.investopedia.com/articles/personal-finance/010616/tax-preparers-vs-financial-advisors-whom-should-you-hire.asp

[43] https://www.thebalance.com/when-you-need-tax-professional-3193494

make him an attractive candidate. However, the lender raised concerns after reviewing his tax returns.

George's tax returns for the past two years showed significant deductions, which had reduced his taxable income considerably. While these deductions were legitimate business expenses, they gave the impression that George's business was less profitable than it actually was.

This discrepancy between the café's actual performance and what was reflected on paper made the lender hesitant to approve the loan, fearing that the business might not generate enough profit to repay the loan.

Understanding the critical role that tax returns play in the loan approval process, we began by conducting a detailed review of George's financial records, including his tax returns, profit and loss statements, and other relevant documents, and identified the key issue. While George had used deductions to minimize his tax liability, these deductions had also inadvertently reduced his reported income to a level that raised concerns for lenders.

To address the situation, we first engaged our Tax Professionals, who reviewed George's tax filings and financial strategy and identified areas where adjustments could be made to present a more accurate and favorable picture of his business's financial health. This included re-evaluating certain deductions and exploring ways to legally optimize George's tax returns without overstating expenses.

Re-adjusting the Tax Returns

Working with our Tax Professional, George decided to amend his tax returns for the previous two years. The amendments were carefully crafted to maintain compliance with tax laws while presenting a more balanced view of his business's profitability. Some deductions were adjusted to better reflect the actual financial situation of the café, resulting in a higher reported income that more accurately depicted the business's success.

Strengthening the Loan Application with Additional Documentation

In addition to the revised tax returns, we advised George to bolster his loan application with supplementary documentation that could further demonstrate the strength and viability of his business. This included detailed cash flow statements, future revenue projections for the new location, and a comprehensive business plan outlining the expansion strategy. We also included testimonials from regular customers and local business partners to emphasize the café's strong community support.

Re-submission and Negotiation with the Lender

With the revised tax returns and additional documentation in hand, George re-submitted his loan application. This time, the lender was able to see a clearer and more accurate representation of the café's financial performance. We also engaged in direct communication with the lender to address any lingering concerns and to clarify how the adjustments in the tax returns were made to more accurately reflect the café's profitability.

Outcome and Client Satisfaction

After reviewing the updated application, the lender approved the loan, allowing George to move forward with his expansion plans. The loan came with favorable terms, reflecting the lender's renewed confidence in George's business.

With the financing secured, George successfully opened his second café location, which quickly became as popular as the first. The expansion not only increased his revenue but also solidified his café's reputation as a staple in the community.

Through this process, George gained a deeper understanding of how tax strategies can impact business financing. The experience showed the importance of balancing tax efficiency with the need to present an accurate picture of financial health to lenders.

By working with us, George was able to overcome the initial challenges and achieve his business expansion goals.

Case Study: Personal Loan for Debt Consolidation

Cindy Roberts, a 32-year-old marketing consultant, had built a successful career working part-time for various companies while also taking on freelance projects. Her diverse income sources provided her with financial flexibility, but they also led to a complex financial situation.

Over time, Cindy accumulated several high-interest debts, including credit card balances and personal loans. Realizing the burden these debts were placing on her finances, she decided to apply for a personal loan to consolidate her debts into a single, lower-interest payment.

When Cindy applied for a personal loan, the lender required her to provide proof of income to assess her ability to repay the loan.

Given her multiple sources of income, the lender requested her recent tax returns as part of the application process. However, Cindy's tax returns were complex and somewhat confusing due to her varied income streams. Her initial tax filings did not clearly represent her total income, leading to discrepancies between her reported earnings and the lender's calculations.

As a result, her loan application was delayed, and the lender requested additional documentation to clarify her financial situation.

Understanding the lender's concerns, we began by conducting a comprehensive review of Cindy's financial situation. We analyzed her tax returns, pay stubs, bank statements, and other financial documents to gain a clear understanding of her actual income and the discrepancies that had caused the lender's concerns. It became evident that while Cindy's income was substantial, the way it was reported in her tax returns did not accurately reflect her financial stability.

Simplification and Clarification of Tax Returns

We simplified and clarified her tax returns as we reviewed her previous filings and identified areas where her income could be more clearly presented. For instance, income from freelance work was consolidated and reported in a manner that was easier for the lender to understand. We also ensured that all income was accurately reported and that any potential discrepancies were addressed.

Re-filing and Supplementing Documentation

We helped Cindy re-file her tax returns to better reflect her true income. The re-filed returns presented a more cohesive and understandable picture of her financial situation.

In addition to the updated tax returns, we advised Cindy to provide the lender with supplementary documentation, including detailed summaries of her freelance contracts, monthly income breakdowns, and a letter explaining the nature of her work and how she managed her finances.

Re-submission of the Loan Application

Armed with the revised tax returns and additional documentation, Cindy re-submitted her personal loan application. The lender now had a clearer understanding of her income and was able to more accurately assess her ability to repay the loan. The clarification provided by the re-filed tax returns and the additional documentation helped dispel the lender's concerns about her financial stability.

After reviewing the updated information, the lender approved Emily's personal loan for debt consolidation. The loan came with a lower interest rate than her previous debts, allowing her to consolidate her high-interest obligations into a single, manageable payment. This not only simplified her financial situation but also saved her money in the long run by reducing the overall interest she would pay.

Emily was relieved to have the financial burden of multiple debts lifted. The experience taught her the importance of clear and accurate financial reporting, especially when dealing with multiple income streams.

Case Study: Business Loan for a Start-Up

Larry Johnson, a tech-savvy entrepreneur with a passion for innovation, had been working on a groundbreaking idea for a tech start-up focused on developing smart home devices.

With a background in software engineering and a strong vision for the future of smart technology, Larry was eager to turn his concept into a reality. However, as a new entrepreneur, he lacked the financial resources necessary to launch his start-up. To secure the funding needed for product development, marketing, and initial operations, he decided to apply for a business loan.

When Larry approached lenders for a business loan, he encountered a significant hurdle. As a new entrepreneur, he had no historical business tax returns or financial records to demonstrate the viability of his start-up.

Without a track record of revenue or profit, lenders were hesitant to approve the loan. They required evidence that Larry's business idea was not only innovative but also financially viable and capable of generating sufficient revenue to repay the loan. The absence of past financial performance made it challenging for him to meet these requirements, putting his start-up plans at risk.

Recognizing that a strong business plan was essential for securing the loan, we began by helping Larry develop a detailed business plan. This plan included an in-depth analysis of the smart home technology market, a clear outline of his business model, and a step-by-step strategy for product development, marketing, and scaling the business. The business plan also highlighted Larry's unique qualifications and expertise in software engineering, positioning him as a credible and capable entrepreneur.

In the absence of historical financial records, we worked with Larry to create realistic and data-driven financial projections. These projections included revenue forecasts, expense estimates, and profitability timelines based on market research and industry benchmarks.

We ensured that the financial projections were aligned with the goals and strategies outlined in the business plan, providing lenders with a clear picture of the potential financial performance of the start-up. The projections also included various scenarios, such as best-case and worst-case outcomes, to demonstrate Larry's preparedness for different market conditions.

Our financial advisors provided valuable insights into the financial aspects of launching a new business and helped refine the financial projections and business plan. They also assisted in preparing additional documentation, such as a detailed breakdown of the start-up costs, a timeline for achieving profitability, and a plan for managing cash flow during the early stages of the business.

Given the lack of business financial history, we advised Larry to supplement his loan application with personal financial information. This included his personal tax returns, credit reports, and a statement of personal assets and liabilities. By providing a complete picture of his personal financial situation, he was able to demonstrate to lenders that he had the financial stability and responsibility to support the start-up during its initial stages. This personal financial information also served as an additional layer of security for the lenders, giving them more confidence in Larry's ability to manage the loan.

With the business plan, financial projections, personal financial information, and additional documentation in hand, we helped Larry prepare and present his loan application to potential lenders. We ensured that the application was clear and well-organized and highlighted the strengths of Larry's business idea, his expertise, and the growth potential of the smart home technology market. We also helped Larry prepare for potential questions or concerns from the lenders, enabling him to confidently address any issues during the loan approval process.

After a thorough review, one of the lenders approved Larry's business loan, recognizing the strength of his business plan and the growth potential of his start-up. The loan provided him with the necessary capital to move forward with product development, marketing, and initial operations.

Within months of launching, Larry's smart home devices gained traction in the market, and the start-up began generating revenue earlier than anticipated. The successful loan application not only enabled Larry to turn his innovative idea into a thriving business but also laid the foundation for future growth and expansion.

Case Study: Mortgage Refinancing for a Retiree

David Anderson, a 68-year-old retiree, had spent his entire career working as an engineer for a major manufacturing company. After decades of hard work, David built a comfortable life for himself and his wife, living in a suburban home that they had owned for over 25 years.

With retirement came a fixed income from his pension, Social Security, and some investment income. As interest rates began to drop, David saw an opportunity to refinance his mortgage, reduce his monthly payments, and free up some cash to enjoy his retirement more comfortably.

When David applied for mortgage refinancing, the lender requested his most recent tax returns to verify his income.

Though David had a stable income from his pension and investments, his initial tax returns did not clearly reflect his financial situation.

The lender had difficulty understanding the various income streams from his pension and investments, leading to concerns about his ability to meet the mortgage payments on a reduced income. This lack of clarity in his tax returns resulted in delays and an initial reluctance from the lender to approve the refinancing application.

Understanding the importance of accurately representing David's financial stability, we started by conducting a comprehensive review of his financial situation.

We analyzed his pension income, Social Security benefits, and investment income to get a clear picture of his total earnings. It became evident that while David's financial situation was stable, the way his income was reported on his tax returns did not fully capture this stability, especially for a lender unfamiliar with the nuances of retirement income.

To address the lender's concerns, we reviewed David's past tax returns and identified areas where the income from his pension and investments could be more clearly presented. We also ensured that any potential discrepancies or ambiguities were resolved to provide a clearer picture of David's financial stability.

We re-filed David's tax returns to more accurately reflect his retirement income. This included separating out the different income streams—pension, Social Security, and investments—and clearly itemizing them on the tax returns. The revised tax returns provided a more straightforward and accurate representation of his financial situation, making it easier for the lender to assess his ability to manage the refinanced mortgage payments.

We also submitted additional documentation to further clarify David's financial stability. This included pension statements, Social Security award letters, and investment account statements, which together provided a comprehensive view of his income sources. We also included a letter explaining the stability of his income and his long history of responsible financial management, further reassuring the lender of his ability to handle the refinanced mortgage.

With the revised tax returns and supplementary documentation, we re-submitted his mortgage refinancing application. This time, the application presented a clear and complete picture of David's financial situation, allowing the lender to accurately assess his ability to repay the loan. The clarity and thoroughness of the documentation helped to alleviate the lender's initial concerns and provided the confidence needed to approve the refinancing.

After reviewing the updated application, the lender approved David's mortgage refinancing, offering him a lower interest rate and reduced monthly payments. This approval provided David with the financial flexibility he was seeking, allowing him to enjoy his retirement with greater peace of mind. The reduced mortgage payments also freed up additional cash flow, which David and his wife used to travel and enjoy their retirement years.

By working with us, David was able to overcome the initial challenges and secure a refinancing deal that significantly improved his financial situation.

Like all these people, we can help you manage your tax returns and get your desired loan approved. We specialize in helping individuals and businesses deal with the complexities of tax returns and financial documentation, just as we have successfully assisted many of our clients in securing loans and mortgages.

Whether you're self-employed, running a small business, or planning for retirement, we can provide you with tailored solutions to ensure that your financial records accurately reflect your stability and potential.

By working closely with you, we help you present the strongest possible case to lenders, increasing your chances of approval and securing the best possible terms for your loan or mortgage. Let us help you achieve your financial goals with confidence and clarity.

Chapter 8: Currently Not Collectible (CNC)

CNC is a tax relief program administered by the Internal Revenue Service (IRS). It is a status assigned to taxpayers who demonstrate that they cannot pay their tax debt. This status pauses collection efforts, allowing taxpayers to focus on stabilizing their financial situation.

The key to qualifying for CNC is demonstrating financial hardship. This means your income is insufficient to cover your basic living expenses and tax debt. Financial hardship can arise from various circumstances, including job loss, illness, or unexpected expenses.[44]

[44] https://www.lexology.com/library/detail.aspx?g=c399abe9-7965-48db-95d2-a9ba8877688f

Eligibility for CNC Status

Taxpayers desiring the Currently Not Collectible status must argue and prove before the IRS that satisfaction of their tax debt would result in a hardship of an extreme nature. Here is an outline to help you determine your eligibility and guide you through meeting the IRS requirements.

Financial Hardship

First and most importantly, one has to prove financial hardship. The IRS has to be able to conclude that paying your tax debt would prevent you from paying your reasonable living expenses. What does that mean?

- **Basic Living Expenses:** Examples of these include rent or mortgage payments, utilities, food, medical care, and transportation. If paying your tax debt means you can't cover these necessities, you may qualify for CNC status.
- **IRS Standards:** The IRS has established guidelines calculating what it considers "necessary" living expenses. This set of guidelines is known as the Collection Financial Standards, and it informs an individual how much can be viewed as the maximum when it comes to food expenses, housing expenses, and transportation expenses, among others, based on one's geographical location and household size. If your expenses are at or below the upper limit of these standards, then your case will be all the more vital.
- **Documentation:** The IRS won't take your word for it. You must provide supporting documentation to validate your assertion of financial hardship. This means submitting such items as:
    - Bank statements of income and expenses
    - Pay stubs or Social Security benefit statements.
    - Utility bills, rent receipts, or mortgage statements.

- Medical bills or statements related to other essential expenses.

This means that you clearly need to paint a picture for the IRS in which, if you pay your tax debt, you will be short on money to pay for your reasonable living expenses.

Filing of Taxes

The second major pre-requisite to achieve CNC status is that you must be current in your tax filings.[45] The IRS will only entertain your request if you have filed returns of prior years. What you should do is as follows:

- **Filing All Tax Returns:** You must have all your tax returns on file and current before applying for CNC, even if a balance is owed on those returns. There is no way around this. The IRS requires all taxpayers filing taxes to comply completely, even those pleading hardship. You'll need to do so now if you haven't filed your taxes on time for any year.
- **Past Due Returns:** If you have unfiled returns from prior years, those must be taken care of before applying for CNC. You can request copies of missing W-2s and 1099s or other documents you need from the IRS by using their transcript service. One needs to file these returns to start becoming compliant.
- **Filing Requirements:** You are still obligated to file timely tax returns in subsequent years after granting CNC status. The IRS will check your filing compliance randomly in subsequent years and may revoke the CNC status for failure to file future returns.

---

[45] https://mdtaxattorney.com/resources/eligible-currently-not-collectible-cnc-status/

Providing Detailed Financial Information

The IRS must conduct a field analysis of your finances to determine whether you are eligible for CNC status. It would help to document your income, expenses, assets, and liabilities. Following are some of the things that the IRS will check:

- **Income:** You must prove every source of your income, including wages, Social Security benefits, pensions, and other income. This can be verified through pay stubs, statements from the Social Security Administration, or bank deposits.
- **Expenses:** The IRS will want to know exactly how much your monthly different expenditures are. This includes:
  - Rent or mortgage payments.
  - Utilities - electricity, water, and gas
  - Food and household expenses
  - Medical expenses, including insurance premiums and out-of-pocket costs
  - Transportation: car payment, insurance, and fuel
- **Assets and Liabilities:** The IRS will also request an inventory of your assets, including bank accounts, property, vehicles, and other valuables. They will compare your assets with your liabilities, such as debts, credit cards, and loans, to assess your financial standing.
- **Documentation:** Supporting documentation for these claims will be required. Such documentation may include:
  - Bank statements outlining your financial transactions.
  - Credit card or loan statements.
  - Valuations on properties or vehicles
  - Medical bills and other proof of necessary expenses

Providing valid and detailed financial documentation is the best way to convince the IRS that you cannot afford your tax bill.

It's not easy to qualify for CNC status, as the IRS sets certain requirements that one needs to fulfill. You can go to bat with the IRS, show financial hardship, be compliant with all tax filings, and provide detailed, substantial financial records. Also, remember that CNC status is temporary and subject to review. For long-term relief from tax collections, a person should maintain compliance.

Case Study: The taxpayer's relief from the IRS on grounds of financial hardship.

Chris, a construction worker, faced a significant setback when he was injured at work, leaving him unable to work for months and consequently falling behind on his taxes. His situation was compounded by several unfiled returns and a growing tax debt. When we stepped in, our professional assistance was instrumental in helping Chris file his overdue returns, prepare detailed financial statements, and demonstrate his financial hardship. Our efforts led to him being granted CNC status, which halted the IRS collection activities.

Avoiding CNC Rejection

One of the biggest obstacles people face when seeking CNC status: non-compliance. Non-compliance typically refers to unfiled tax returns, and it's a problem because the IRS will not consider granting CNC status unless you are fully compliant with all of your filings.

This can be a significant roadblock if you've fallen behind on filing in past years. The IRS takes tax compliance very seriously, so if you have even one unfiled return, you must get that sorted before CNC status is even possible. I know this sounds overwhelming, especially if you have multiple years of unfiled returns. But here is the thing—you don't have to tackle this alone. I have catered to many clients in this exact situation, and with the proper guidance, they got back on track.

The best approach is to work methodically to get those returns filed. If you're missing some documentation from prior years, like W-2s or 1099s, don't worry—you can request transcripts from the IRS, which will give you the data you need to file those returns. Catching up on unfiled returns can feel daunting, but it is a crucial first step toward resolving your tax debt.

This is where a tax professional, such as an Enrolled Agent (EA), CPA, or tax attorney, can be invaluable. They can help you gather the necessary documentation, ensure accurate returns, and even file them on your behalf.[46] With professional help, you can make sure that every detail is handled correctly, and you avoid the risk of further mistakes that could lead to penalties or audits down the line.

Failure to address past-due returns and other compliance matters can significantly hinder the IRS's willingness to consider a taxpayer's request for relief. By ensuring that all outstanding obligations are met, individuals can significantly enhance their chances of successfully securing CNC status and effectively managing their tax debt.

Navigating the CNC Process: A Step-by-Step Guide

The first step is filing any overdue tax returns. If you are behind on your filings, the IRS won't even consider your application for CNC. Many people panic about filing several years' worth of returns but trust me—there's no way around it. The good news is that the sooner you file, the sooner you can move forward with your CNC request.

Here's how you can tackle those overdue returns:

[46] https://www.plunkettcooney.com/dontbetthebusinessblog/currently-non-collectible-status

1. **Gather all your income documentation**: This includes W-2s, 1099s, and other income records for the years you have not filed. If you do not have some documents, don't worry—you can request a transcript from the IRS showing the income reported under your Social Security number.
2. **Review deductions and credits**: Be thorough. Any deductions or credits you qualify for will help reduce the amount you owe, and that is important when you're trying to demonstrate financial hardship.
3. **File the returns**: You can file electronically for most years or submit paper returns for older tax years. The goal here is to get caught up, plain and simple.[47]

Once your tax returns are filed, the next step is preparing detailed financial statements. You must show the IRS that paying your tax debt would put you in a difficult financial position. Here's what the IRS is looking for:

1. **Income**: They will want to know your total monthly income from all sources, including wages, Social Security, pensions, and any other income streams.
2. **Expenses**: You must provide a detailed breakdown of your essential living expenses. This includes rent or mortgage, utilities, food, transportation, medical expenses, and other costs necessary for daily living.
3. **Assets**: The IRS will also want to know about your assets, including any property you own, bank accounts, vehicles, or other valuable assets.

The more organized and detailed your financial statements, the stronger your case. The IRS uses this information to determine whether you can pay your tax debt reasonably. Your argument for

---

[47] https://www.accounting.com/resources/how-to-do-taxes/

CNC status strengthens if your necessary living expenses leave little to no disposable income[48].

But this documentation can be tricky to compile on your own. That is why it's essential to consider professional help. Filing your overdue returns and submitting detailed financial statements can get complicated, and that's where tax professionals come in.

Role of Tax Professionals in CNC Cases

Tax professionals like CPAs, Enrolled Agents (EAs), and tax attorneys play a crucial role in making sure everything is done correctly and efficiently when it comes to CNC cases.

A tax professional will assist you in organizing all the necessary documents. If your tax returns are unfiled or incomplete, they will help you gather the required information and file them on your behalf. But beyond just filing paperwork, they will ensure your returns are accurate and that you've claimed all the deductions and credits available to you. This alone can significantly reduce the tax debt you owe.

When it comes to financial statements, a professional will know how to structure and present your financial information to strengthen your case. Remember, the IRS has specific guidelines and thresholds for determining financial hardship, and learning how to present your income, expenses, and assets correctly is critical. A tax professional will work closely with you to ensure every detail is accounted for.[49]

Once your documents are ready, your tax professional will negotiate directly with the IRS on your behalf. The IRS can be difficult to deal with, especially if you don't know the ins and outs of the tax code, but professionals are trained to handle these negotiations. They will represent you in discussions about your

---

48 https://vintti.com/blog/navigating-tax-season-a-step-by-step-guide/
49 https://cepr.org/voxeu/columns/true-role-tax-professionals

CNC status, ensuring your case is presented clearly and accurately. This can significantly reduce stress, and it's often the difference between success and failure in securing CNC status.

For instance, a single mom, Kelly, came to us in a bad financial situation. Her small business went under, leaving her with much debt and prohibiting her from paying taxes. She had several unfiled returns and was overwhelmed completely.

First, we worked to get Kelly back in compliance by filing all her back returns and sorting out her financial records. Because Kelly had no sense of her current economic situation, working with her to compile all the resources: income, expenses, and any assets she still possessed was necessary. We then outlined these in a manner that showed her financial hardship.

Once she had filed her returns and provided her financial statements, we took over the negotiations with the IRS and proved that Kelly could not pay her tax debt without sacrificing her family's well-being. Based on our documentation, the IRS granted Kelly CNC status, meaning they stopped all collection efforts.

But that wasn't the end of our work. CNC status is temporary, so we kept working with Kelly to develop a financial plan to keep her compliant. This underscores the importance of long-term financial planning, a service we provide to ensure our clients do not find themselves in the same predicament.

Briefly, going through this process with a tax professional guarantees that everything is right the first time. We know the IRS's process for working complex cases, and more importantly, our expertise provides you with the reassurance that we can present your case in the most robust possible way to give you the best chance of success.

How to maintain your CNC status?

Once you obtain CNC status, continuing compliance with the tax laws will be necessary. The IRS expects you to keep current on filing your taxes. You will need to file all future tax returns on time. If you fail to do so-even missing just one deadline may lead to severe consequences and a possible loss of your CNC status.

It's a common scenario: individuals celebrate being granted CNC status, only to have their subsequent filings arrive late or not at all. The IRS scrutinizes the files of taxpayers with CNC status, and a single compliance error could jeopardize the CNC status. Timely filing of tax returns is a clear demonstration of good faith and is crucial to maintaining your standing.[50]

Besides that, the IRS will periodically check your financial status during your CNC status. They will have to be assured that your situation has not changed. And if they believe you can now start paying the debt, they'll take action. So, stay compliant, file those returns, and don't worsen a bad situation.

Risks of CNC Revocation

It's crucial to meet your compliance obligations to avoid the revocation of your CNC status. Once that happens, the IRS can resume collection actions, and the consequences are severe. They can levy your bank accounts, garnish your wages, or even place liens on your property. This is a situation you want to avoid at all costs.

For instance, Phillip became complacent after proving his financial hardship and being granted the status of CNC. He did not file his next tax return on time because he knew he didn't have much money coming in and didn't think it was a big deal. Well, the IRS noticed and promptly removed his CNC status. Just like that, Phillip once again found himself in the crosshairs of the IRS-

---

[50] https://choicetaxrelief.com/tax-relief/currently-not-collectible-status/

the IRS- the collection efforts the CNC designed to protect him from.

When Phillip came to us, his situation had escalated, and he was desperate. First, we helped him file the delinquent returns to get him back into compliance. We then worked directly with the IRS to prove that his non-compliance was only a one-time mistake and that his financial situation had yet to improve. After some negotiation with the IRS, we could reinstate his CNC status again and give Phillip the relief he needed.[51]

The lesson is clear here: *Do not let non-compliance undermine the good work. Be vigilant and ensure that your tax obligations are complied with. This vigilance will empower you and ensure you do not inadvertently lose the benefits of the CNC status.*

Case Study: How Chris Made It Big with CNC

Chris was a hardworking construction worker in a difficult situation following a terrible injury. Out of work for many months, his income took a severe nosedive. To make matters worse, he had not filed his tax returns in several years. His financial situation continued spiralling, and the IRS knocked on his door.

When Chris first came to me, he was rightfully anxious. He had a mountain of tax debt and several unfiled returns and needed a clear idea about how to fix this. First, I told him we needed to take care of those unfiled returns immediately. The IRS will not consider CNC status if you are not current with your tax filings.

First, we filed his back returns. Chris was too scared to file because of the penalties; I had to reassure him that this was the next step. We gathered his income information from several years,

---

[51] https://www.irs.gov/businesses/small-businesses-self-employed/revocation-or-denial-of-passport-in-cases-of-certain-unpaid-taxes

including W-2s and 1099s. I helped get it all together and submitted it. After filing those returns, we could work on proving he had financial hardship.

Chris's injury had taken away most of his savings, and his medical bills kept piling up. We prepared detailed financial statements showing his income, necessary living expenses, and assets. This showed the IRS that paying his tax debt would leave him unable to meet basic living expenses. Having laid out his financial situation, we submitted his CNC request.

The IRS granted Chris' request, placing him into CNC status. All collection efforts were stopped, and he received the breathing room he desperately needed to recover. The Story of Chris reminds one that no matter how impossible the situation may appear, there is always a way forward if the approach is correct.

Case Study: Kelly's Tax Debt Relief

Kelly, a single mom running a small business that had recently gone under. The collapse had put her in financial ruin: colossal debt and no clue how to pay taxes. She had never known how to keep her finances straight, so all her records were a real mess.

Kelly was most concerned with how the IRS would react to her situation and thus came to me in a panic. First, I had her take a few deep breaths and know there was a course of action. The organization would be essential for Kelly, who must file her returns and document her financial hardship.

We started by going through her finances in great detail. Since Kelly needed to figure out how much she owed to the IRS, we helped her recreate her financial records. We filed her back returns, ensuring every piece of income and every allowable deduction was included. This was a necessary step to avoid further penalties or issues.

Next, we worked on compiling the financial statements that would show the IRS her dire situation: With no steady income, no assets to fall back on, and two children to take care of, Kelly clearly could not pay any tax debt. I made sure her documentation was tight, pointing out exactly what her income was, what her monthly expenses were, and what few remaining assets she did have.

Once we had all the material submitted, we proceeded to negotiate with the IRS. We requested CNC status based on her current financial hardship, citing that any attempts to force her to pay her tax debt would put her family's well-being in jeopardy. After the IRS reviewed our CNC status request, they granted Kelly this status and ceased all collection activity.

Kelly was relieved. Although the CNC was only a temporary solution, it gave her time and space to sort herself out and plan her next moves. We continued working together and set her up with a better system for managing finances and ensuring ongoing compliance.

Kelly's Story is an ideal example of hesitating to seek professional help to deal with the IRS. Proper guidance and an organized approach will help you solve even the most complicated case.

Financial Documentation for Taxpayers Seeking CNC Status

Financial documentation plays a pivotal role when seeking CNC status. The IRS relies on these records to determine whether paying your tax debt would cause undue hardship. I always stress the importance of keeping accurate, detailed financial records. Every dollar you earn and expense you have needs to be documented clearly and consistently.

Start by maintaining a comprehensive record of your monthly income and expenses. This includes pay stubs, utility bills, medical expenses, and bank statements. The IRS will scrutinize this data, which must be thorough and up to date. I also recommend creating a system for tracking your assets and liabilities—knowing where you stand financially is critical for the CNC process and overall financial health[52].

Good record-keeping shows the IRS that you are serious about managing your finances and meeting your obligations, even if you can't pay your tax debt. It is one of the most critical aspects of successfully securing CNC status.

Long-Term Planning After Getting CNC Status

Currently, Not Collectible can be a huge relief. You probably already celebrated the day this status was granted, feeling like a weight had been lifted off your shoulders. However, it is essential to understand that CNC is not permanent—it only pauses the IRS collection efforts but does not wipe out your tax debt. Therefore, long-term planning cannot be understated to avoid future financial strains and clear your tax obligations.

Scoping Other Options for Tax Relief

Once this status is secured, I first advise my clients to begin exploring permanent tax relief options such as an Offer in Compromise or an Installment Agreement. These are more permanent solutions to settle your tax debt once and for all.

Offer in Compromise:

The OIC will allow you to negotiate with the IRS and settle your tax debt for less than you owe. This is ideal in those cases where one can prove that paying the total amount is impossible due to one's financial status. The IRS uses one's income, expense,

[52] https://www.sambrotman.com/the-complete-guide-to-irs-collections/what-if-cannot-pay-irs/#:~:text=Qualifying%20for%20CNC%20status%20is,before%20taxes%20and%20other%20deductions.

and asset equity as qualification bases. If you can prove that paying your total tax debt would be a great hardship, then an OIC may be the proper alternative for you. However, it has to be remembered that an OIC application is complex in nature and requires detailed documentation to be effective.

Installment Agreement:

When an OIC is not feasible, an installment agreement could be used. In this case, one can pay their tax debt in manageable monthly installments. An Installment Agreement is much easier to qualify for than an OIC, and it provides taxpayers with a systematic means of paying off their debt over time without heavily denting their pocketbooks. While interest and penalties will still accrue on the outstanding balance, the Installment Agreement does eliminate aggressive IRS collection efforts, such as a levy or wage garnishment.

The sooner these are explored, the better your financial stability will be in the long term. Both the solutions provide a path toward permanent resolution of your tax issues, which should be your ultimate goal.[53]

Importance of Proactive Financial Management

While CNC status provides temporary relief, proactive financial planning is essential to prevent future tax problems. The last thing you need or want is to face the same situation again. What I recommend for my clients once they have obtained CNC status is as follows:

Budget Development:

One of the most beneficial ways to help you avoid future tax problems is by establishing a budget that clearly depicts your

---

53 https://deepblue.lib.umich.edu/bitstream/handle/2027.42/169865/stuartem_1.pdf?sequence=1

income, expenses, and balanced tax liabilities. Most taxpayers fall behind during the year due to needing more time to plan ahead of time for taxes, especially in the case of self-employed individuals. You can avoid creating new tax debt by making this kind of incorporation within your budget.

Increasing Income or Reducing Expenses:

The CNC status does not eliminate the debt but temporarily halts its collection. To improve your financial standing, consolidate your income or cut unnecessary spending. Even the smallest changes add up significantly over time. Additional money coming in or money saved by cutting down on expenses can be used to pad your account, making struggling with tax debt easier when the time to face the problem approaches.

Exploring Debt Consolidation Options:

Besides your tax liability, if you have any other forms of debt, then debt consolidation can help. High-interest debt can be consolidated into a lower-interest loan. This frees up the money used to service high-interest loans and makes the money available to settle your taxes. A tax professional or financial advisor can help you decide if this is a good option.

Benefits and Limitations of CNC Status

While CNC status can have its temporary beneficial points, it is equally important to understand what limitations and advantages come with it:

Benefits:

CNC status temporarily stops IRS collection methods applied to create pressure for payment, including wage garnishment, bank levies, and seizures of property. In a sense, it's an immediate saving grace since you'll be able to catch your breath as you begin rebuilding your finances. This allows the time needed to reorganize finances free from continuous pressure applied by IRS collections.

Limitations:

The IRS will check your finances occasionally, and it may revoke the CNC status and start collecting if your financial situation improves. Meanwhile, while you enjoy CNC status, the underlying tax debt continues to accrue interest and penalties over time, increasing the total amount owed.

Long-Term Planning

While CNC status can take time, you must take steps towards a permanent solution. Failure to plan could put you back in the hole once the CNC status is lifted. There are some things that can be done to avoid that:

Stay Compliant with Future Tax Filings:

You must file your tax returns every year on time, even on CNC status. If you don't, the IRS may revoke your CNC status and start collecting again. It just shows to the IRS that you are compliant with filing your taxes, although you cannot pay at that moment.

Monitor Your Financial Situation Regularly:

Having a set budget will keep you from being behind. Take some time each month to compare your income and expenses and make changes as your financial situation changes. This will keep you ahead in your finances and allow you to make the adjustments you need.

Meet with a Tax Professional:

Working through CNC status and thinking about the future can sometimes be challenging. One of the best things you can do is to consult a tax professional who will ensure that you are taking the proper steps. A tax professional can consider long-term options with you, prepare the necessary documents, and help facilitate the application process for other available tax relief programs like an OIC or Installment Agreement.

The Path to Long-Term Financial Stability

While CNC status provides much-needed relief for taxpayers in financial hardship, it's only temporary. You must be more proactive in finding permanent tax relief options, complying with future tax filings, and occasionally monitoring your financial situation.[54] You can resolve your tax debt and prevent further financial difficulties with proper planning and the help of a tax professional.

---

[54] https://www.hrblock.com/tax-center/irs/audits-and-tax-notices/how-to-get-currently-not-collectible/

Chapter 9: Government Benefits

Non-compliance with tax filings is far more than a matter of potential fines or interest—it has profound implications on your ability to access essential government benefits. When taxpayers fail to file their returns, they often overlook the long-term impact on their financial stability and well-being. Many benefits that provide financial security for individuals and families—such as Social Security, healthcare subsidies, student loans, and tax credits—are tied directly to the information reported in your tax filings. But, without those filings, the government cannot assess your eligibility for these critical programs.

For example, your Social Security benefits are calculated based on the earnings you report on your tax returns throughout your working years. If you file, your earnings history is complete, potentially reducing your future retirement income. Similarly, healthcare subsidies provided under the Affordable Care Act (ACA) rely on your tax return to determine the amount of financial assistance you're eligible for. Without filing, you could lose these essential subsidies, leading to higher healthcare costs.[55]

For students, particularly those from low- to middle-income families, access to federal financial aid through the Free Application for Federal Student Aid (FAFSA) requires up-to-date tax filings. Your eligibility for grants, loans, and work-study programs is protected without this information. Failing to file tax returns disrupts access to these benefits and can create onerous financial burdens to recover from.

Importance of Filing Tax Returns

It is essential to understand that filing your tax returns is not just about paying taxes. Even if you don't owe any taxes or are due a refund, filing remains critical to staying compliant with

---

[55] https://www.irs.gov/taxpayer-bill-of-rights

federal and state laws. More importantly, it is the foundation upon which eligibility for many government benefits is built.

When you fail to file, you risk penalties and interest and jeopardize your access to benefits that can provide long-term financial support. These include Social Security and healthcare subsidies, the Child Tax Credit (CTC), and the Earned Income Tax Credit (EITC), which provide significant financial relief to low- and moderate-income households.[56] Filing your tax returns on time ensures you maintain eligibility for these benefits, protecting your financial future and your family.

Social Security Benefits

Impact on Social Security Contributions

When it comes to securing your financial future, Social Security benefits are critical. However, many taxpayers, particularly the self-employed—fail to realize how not filing their tax returns can seriously impact the calculation of these benefits. As an expert in U.S. taxation, let me explain how the IRS and the Social Security Administration (SSA) work together to calculate your future benefits and why maintaining compliance with your tax filings is essential.

For self-employed people, you are responsible for paying both the employer and employee portions of Social Security and Medicare taxes, often referred to as self-employment taxes. These payments are reported on your tax returns and are crucial to how the SSA calculates your earnings history.[57] Your Social Security contributions are based directly on the income you report to the IRS, so if you're not filing your returns, you are not reporting your

---

[56]https://www.irs.gov/newsroom/who-needs-to-file-a-tax-return#:~:text=Avoid%20interest%20and%20penalties.,extension%20to%20avoid%20some%20penalties.

[57] https://www.irs.gov/faqs/social-security-income

income. Thus, your contributions to Social Security aren't being credited.

The SSA uses your reported income from these tax filings to determine the Average Indexed Monthly Earnings (AIME). This figure is vital in calculating your monthly benefits after retirement. If your income isn't reported because of unfiled tax returns, the SSA will have incomplete data, leading to lower future benefits or, in some cases, no benefits. This can be devastating for individuals relying on Social Security as their primary source of retirement income.[58]

In short, failing to file your tax returns deprives the SSA of the information needed to calculate your benefits correctly. If you are self-employed and haven't filed, you're not just avoiding taxes but jeopardizing your future financial security. It is a mistake that may not show immediate consequences, but it will profoundly impact you when you reach retirement age.

Case Study: Maxine

Maxine was a freelance consultant with a small, relatively stable income for many years. Unfortunately, she didn't feel the need to file her tax returns regularly since her income fluctuated, and sometimes, she needed to figure out how much she owed.

By the time she came to us, Maxine had multiple years of unfiled returns and reached an age not far from retirement. She was shocked that the SSA had incomplete earnings records when she applied for her Social Security benefits. This was not the SSA's mistake; Maxine had never reported her self-employment income to the IRS; hence, it didn't get to the SSA for its benefit calculations.

We immediately took action. Our first step was to help Maxine file all her overdue tax returns. When we filed those

---

[58] https://www-origin.ssa.gov/benefits/retirement/planner/taxes.html

returns, her earnings history was updated correctly with the IRS and then reflected in the SSA's records, ensuring her total contributions were accounted for. With her financial records corrected, Maxine's future Social Security benefits were restored properly, preserving her retirement income.

It is an ideal example of how tax compliance may affect long-term benefits. She did not file and inadvertently limited her capacity to claim the full benefits she accrued. Fortunately, we were able to sort that out, but it is a good lesson learned about how important filing current taxes is.

Implications for Future Retirement

The consequences of not filing your tax returns extend far beyond just potential penalties from the IRS—they can have a lasting impact on your retirement benefits. For most Americans, Social Security is a primary source of income in retirement, and any reduction in benefits due to incomplete earnings records can be financially catastrophic.

If your tax returns are filed on time, the SSA receives the information to calculate your benefits accurately. This means the benefits you're entitled to could be significantly reduced. The SSA relies entirely on the earnings you report to the IRS to calculate your AIME, which determines the monthly benefits you will receive. If you fail to report your income, or if the income you report is less than your actual earnings due to incomplete or unfiled returns, your AIME will be lower than it should be, resulting in smaller payments once you retire.[59]

Additionally, there is a time limit for correcting unfiled returns and ensuring your income is reported to the SSA. If too much time passes, you may lose the opportunity to fix these errors,

---

[59] https://www.irs.gov/retirement-plans/plan-sponsor/benefits-of-setting-up-a-retirement-plan

leaving you permanently shortchanged. In Maxine's case, we rectified the issue because we acted promptly, but this window of opportunity can close, making it impossible to recover lost benefits.

This risk is even higher for self-employed individuals because they are responsible for reporting their income and paying self-employment taxes. With those filings, the IRS and SSA can know how much revenue was earned and how much should be credited toward retirement. Many self-employed taxpayers think skipping a tax filing one year won't make a difference, but in reality, every year of non-filing reduces your future retirement benefits.[60]

Failing to file your tax returns is about more than just the immediate consequences of dealing with the IRS. It is about safeguarding your long-term financial health. By ensuring that your income is accurately reported each year, you stay compliant with the IRS, protect your Social Security benefits, and ensure your retirement years are financially secure. The lesson here is clear: Stay on top of your tax filings, and don't risk your future financial well-being by neglecting this critical responsibility.

Health Insurance and the Affordable Care Act (ACA)

Eligibility for Health Insurance Subsidies

Health insurance subsidies under the Affordable Care Act (ACA) are crucial for many Americans who need access to affordable healthcare. These subsidies, known as Premium Tax Credits, are designed to reduce the monthly premium costs for individuals and families with low to moderate incomes. However, many people need to realize that eligibility for these subsidies is directly tied to the income reported on your tax returns.

---

60 https://www.ml.com/articles/taxes-in-retirement.html

The IRS and the Health Insurance Marketplace work together to determine your subsidy eligibility. When you apply for health insurance through the Marketplace, the information you provide about your income is cross-referenced with the income reported on your most recent tax return. This income data is critical because it helps calculate your household income as a percentage of the federal poverty level (FPL). If your income falls between 100% and 400% of the FPL, you may be eligible for subsidies that lower your monthly premium payments.[61]

If you fail to file your tax returns or the income you report is inaccurate, the Marketplace cannot verify your subsidy eligibility. This could result in two major issues: first, you could be denied the subsidy altogether, meaning you will pay the total price for your health insurance premiums. Second, if you initially received a subsidy based on an estimated income but later failed to file your tax return, the IRS can require you to repay part or all of that subsidy.

For individuals and families who rely on these subsidies to afford healthcare, the importance of tax compliance cannot be overstated. Filing your returns on time and ensuring that your income is accurately reported is essential to maintaining eligibility for these critical benefits. In essence, your tax return not only affects your tax liability but can also significantly impact your healthcare costs.[62]

Case Study: Carol

Carol's story perfectly shows how failing to file tax returns can lead to immediate and costly consequences on healthcare. Carol qualified for Premium Tax Credits under the ACA as a self-employed graphic designer. She didn't file her tax returns for two years because she was busy and unsure of her income. She lost the

[61] https://www.irs.gov/affordable-care-act
[62] https://www.irs.gov/taxtopics/tc763

subsidy for health insurance and had to pay the total price for her insurance premiums, which significantly burdened her finances.

When Carol came to us, she didn't even realize that she had forgotten to file some taxes, which was the reason for her inflated healthcare costs. We helped her quickly assemble all the documents and file her delinquent taxes. Now that the income was reported correctly, we could claim the subsidies she had missed retroactively. This significantly reduced her cost of health care; the Marketplace recalculated her eligibility and applied the credits to which she was entitled.

Carol's case shows that compliance with tax filings is essential, as it could ensure access to affordable health care; without professional intervention, she would have been paying much higher premiums than required.

Consequences of Non-Compliance

Failing to file your tax returns doesn't just affect your standing with the IRS—it can also have immediate financial consequences in other areas, particularly when it comes to healthcare. When you lose access to Premium Tax Credits due to non-compliance, you are responsible for paying the total cost of your health insurance premiums. This can be a significant financial burden for many individuals and families, making healthcare unaffordable or forcing them to forego coverage entirely.

The cost of losing subsidies can be severe. Depending on your plan and income level, premiums can increase by hundreds or even thousands of dollars annually.[63] This can quickly drain your finances, making it difficult to choose between paying for healthcare and other essential living expenses.

---

[63] https://www.irs.gov/charities-non-profits/consequence-of-non-compliance-with-section-501r

Moreover, once you lose your eligibility for subsidies, reinstating them can be a time-consuming process. You must file all overdue tax returns and ensure your income is accurately reported. Even after that, it may take time for the Marketplace to adjust your subsidies.

Non-compliance with tax filings can immediately and detrimentally impact your financial ability to access healthcare. Staying compliant ensures continued access to these valuable subsidies and manages healthcare costs.

Federal Student Loans and Financial Aid

Tax Filing and FAFSA Eligibility

In the U.S., access to federal student loans and grants depends heavily on accurate and timely tax filings. The Free Application for Federal Student Aid (FAFSA), the primary form used to apply for federal financial aid, requires detailed information about a family's income and assets. This information is pulled directly from the most recent tax return the student or their parents filed.[64] Therefore, if tax returns are current, it can ensure a student's eligibility for federal aid.

The IRS Data Retrieval Tool (DRT), a feature within the FAFSA application, allows the IRS to provide tax return data directly to the U.S. Department of Education. This ensures that the financial information used to assess needs is accurate. However, if the tax returns are not filed, the DRT cannot function, and the FAFSA application will either be delayed or incomplete. This could mean missing crucial deadlines and, in turn, missing out on essential financial aid for college education.[65]

---

[64] https://www.irs.gov/newsroom/reminder-educational-assistance-programs-can-help-pay-workers-student-loans
[65] https://www.irs.gov/individuals/students

Failing to file tax returns can delay the processing of FAFSA applications and disqualify students from receiving grants, loans, or work-study programs. As an expert, I cannot stress enough the importance of ensuring that all tax filings are current before submitting a FAFSA application.

Case Study: The Johnson Family

The Johnson family faced this issue when they should have filed their tax returns for several years. Their son was about to start college and had completed his FAFSA application, but his application was incomplete due to the lack of tax filings. As a result, his financial aid package was delayed, putting his college plans at risk.

The family sought our help, and we immediately assisted them in filing their overdue returns. Once those returns are processed, the IRS Data Retrieval Tool can provide the financial information to the FAFSA system. Within weeks, their son's financial assistance package was approved, and he secured the required grants and loans for college. This case illustrates how timely tax filings are essential for securing educational opportunities.

Financial Impact on Families

The financial impact of failing to file tax returns extends beyond just missing out on federal aid. Delays in the FAFSA process can lead to increased out-of-pocket expenses, higher interest rates on private loans, or even a complete loss of federal grants, which do not need to be repaid. In many cases, students relying on federal aid to attend college could face severe educational disruptions if their families do not comply with tax filings.

Families must recognize that tax compliance affects their children's education and financial future. By staying current with tax filings, they ensure students have the financial resources to pursue higher education without unnecessary delays or financial burdens. This proactive approach prevents missed opportunities and helps secure the future of their children's educational journeys.

Veterans' Benefits

Income Verification for Veterans' Benefits

For veterans, maintaining disability and pension benefits often depends on accurate income reporting through tax filings. The Department of Veterans Affairs (VA) uses income data from tax returns to verify eligibility for certain benefits, especially those that are means-tested, like the VA pension or needs-based disability compensation. Veterans may face reduced benefits or even lose their eligibility if income is reported correctly due to unfiled tax returns; for example, some veterans qualify for VA pensions based on income.[66] If tax returns are not filed, the VA cannot verify the veteran's income levels, which could result in either an overpayment that needs to be repaid later or an underpayment in which the veteran does not receive the full benefits they are entitled. Other programs, like the Aid and Attendance benefit, which assists veterans with long-term care needs, rely on income verification through tax filings.

Compliance with tax filings is not just a requirement for financial aid—veterans need to maintain the full scope of the benefits they deserve after serving their country.[67]

Case Study: Mike

A decorated Army veteran, Michael suddenly found his VA disability benefits drastically reduced, thus creating much financial hardship. When calling the VA, he found his income had

---

[66] https://www.irs.gov/individuals/military/special-tax-considerations-for-veterans
[67] https://www.irs.gov/individuals/information-for-veterans

been reduced because the Veterans Affairs office could not verify his income from unfiled tax returns. Due to the inability to verify his income properly, Mike's benefits were changed and recalculated based on incomplete information.

Knowing he needed professional assistance, Mike came to us for help. We assisted him in filing his back returns and reporting all income information to the IRS and VA. After he caught up, the VA reinstated his full benefits, and he regained his financial security. Mike's case indicates the need for updated tax filings since this document serves as proof of benefits eligibility and income for veterans.

Ensuring Continuity of Benefits

Veterans must prioritize tax compliance to ensure uninterrupted access to the benefits they have earned. Please file tax returns that affect current payments and can lead to the need for retroactive adjustments or repayment of overpaid benefits. Veterans who fall behind on tax filings risk losing critical support, including healthcare, pensions, and long-term care assistance.

Regularly reviewing and updating tax filings is crucial for veterans who receive means-tested benefits. By ensuring that income is accurately reported and all returns are filed on time, veterans can protect themselves from unexpected benefit reductions or cancellations. Additionally, staying compliant with tax obligations reduces the risk of audits or disputes with the IRS, allowing veterans to focus on their health and well-being rather than worrying about their financial security.

Child Tax Credit (CTC) and Earned Income Tax Credit (EITC)

Significance of CTC and EITC

The Child Tax Credit (CTC) and Earned Income Tax Credit (EITC) are two of the most valuable financial tools available to low- and moderate-income families. These credits can offer substantial financial relief by reducing your overall tax liability and, in some cases, resulting in a refund. However, as an expert, I cannot emphasize enough how tax compliance is critical to ensuring you can take full advantage of these credits.[68]

You must file your tax returns to avoid falling behind with the IRS and forfeiting the opportunity to claim these credits. Both the CTC and EITC require annual tax filings to determine eligibility. The IRS uses the information you provide in your tax return to calculate the amount you are eligible to receive.[69] If you do not file, tell the IRS you are not interested in receiving these benefits. For families struggling to make ends meet, this can result in a significant loss of income that could otherwise help cover basic expenses such as food, housing, and childcare.

Moreover, the IRS requires taxpayers claiming the EITC to meet specific income thresholds, which are assessed based on the income reported on their tax return. If you file, the IRS cannot provide verifiability, and you miss out on the substantial relief the EITC can provide. Similarly, the Child Tax Credit, designed to support families raising children, can offer up to $2,000 per qualifying child, but again, this requires a proper filing of your tax returns each year.

Failing to file tax returns results in the loss of these credits for the current year and prior years if you fall behind on your filings. Low- and moderate-income families can ensure they receive these credits' full benefits by maintaining compliance.

Case Study: Steven's Story

Steven was a middle-aged restaurant manager who had never realized how essential tax filings put money in his pocket. Single,

---

[68] https://www.irs.gov/credits-deductions/individuals/child-tax-credit
[69] https://www.irs.gov/credits-deductions/individuals/earned-income-tax-credit-eitc

with no children of his own, Steven thought little about filing taxes on the Child Tax Credit and Earned Income Tax Credit. But when his sister and brother-in-law died unexpectedly, Steven was suddenly a single caregiver to their two young nieces. Overnight, he became eligible for not one credit but both.

Steven had not filed his taxes in many years and had never applied for these tax credits, which could have helped him financially. Raising two children was expensive, and he had difficulty paying for everyday expenses because he had never filed his returns. The unresolved accumulation of unfiled returns overwhelmed him, and he didn't realize all the benefits he'd lost.

The minute Steven contacted our office, we helped him file his delinquent tax returns and adequately document the guardianship of his nieces. It wasn't until Steven became compliant with the IRS through filing that he could finally claim the CTC for the nieces and qualify for the EITC for himself, providing significant financial relief. These credits helped lighten the burden of raising his nieces and gave Steven the peace of mind that his tax situation was finally square with the IRS.

Financial Relief for Low-Income Families

The Child Tax Credit (CTC) and Earned Income Tax Credit (EITC) are two of the most potent financial relief programs available to low- and moderate-income families. These credits can drastically reduce tax liabilities or result in a substantial refund, providing much-needed economic support for families living paycheck to paycheck. For many households, these credits can make the difference between being able to afford necessities and struggling to make ends meet.

For example, the EITC is particularly beneficial for low-income families, as it can increase their income by up to several thousand dollars per year. Similarly, the CTC provides up to $2,000 per child, helping parents or guardians cover the costs of raising children, such as school supplies, childcare, and healthcare. However, these benefits are only available to those who are compliant with their tax filings.

Maintaining tax compliance is essential to ensuring continued eligibility for these credits. Filing on time yearly guarantees that low-income families receive the financial assistance they are entitled to, helping them achieve more excellent economic stability.[70] By working with tax professionals, families can avoid missing out on these critical benefits and ensure that they remain in good standing with the IRS.

The Broader Impact of Non-Compliance

The Critical Role of Tax Compliance

Tax compliance is not just about avoiding penalties from the IRS; it plays a crucial role in securing your long-term financial well-being. Non-compliance with tax filings can lead to the loss of critical government benefits that many families rely on for economic stability. These benefits, including Social Security, healthcare subsidies, student loans, and tax credits, are designed to provide a safety net. However, they are only available to those who maintain up-to-date and accurate tax filings.[71]

Please file your tax returns on time so the IRS and other government agencies can adequately assess your eligibility for these programs. This can result in reduced or delayed Social Security benefits during retirement, loss of Premium Tax Credits under the ACA, ineligibility for federal student aid, and forfeiture of vital tax credits like the CTC and EITC. The consequences of non-compliance reach far beyond the immediate financial penalties; they can fundamentally undermine your financial future.

---

[70] https://www.irs.gov/advocate/low-income-taxpayer-clinics
[71] https://www.irs.gov/pub/irs-soi/bloomquist.pdf

Encouraging Compliance

As an expert in U.S. taxation and financial law, I encourage you to seek professional assistance if you've fallen behind on your tax filings. The sooner you address the issue, the better your chances of protecting your access to essential government programs. Working with a tax professional can ensure that your filings are accurate, complete, and submitted on time, thereby safeguarding your eligibility for the benefits that can provide both short-term relief and long-term financial security.

It is always possible to get back into compliance. Whether you are self-employed, unsure how to handle past returns, or you've fallen behind, taking proactive steps now can prevent a cascade of negative consequences. Professional assistance can guide you through the process, helping you navigate any complexities or uncertainties with your tax filings.

The importance of tax compliance cannot be overstated. Filing your tax returns on time is not just a legal obligation but a fundamental step toward protecting your financial future. Government programs like Social Security, healthcare subsidies, and student aid are designed to support you during critical moments in your life, but they require ongoing compliance with tax laws. Failure to file puts these benefits at risk, leaving you vulnerable to financial hardship.[72]

Take immediate action if you need to catch up on your filings. By filing your overdue returns, you ensure you remain eligible for the benefits that can make a significant difference in your life. Inaction costs are far too high regarding lost benefits and long-term financial instability. Compliance with tax laws is about avoiding penalties and ensuring access to the programs supporting your financial well-being.

---

72 https://www.irs.gov/statistics/compliance-presence

Chapter 10: Passport and Driver's License Issues

The repercussions of tax non-compliance are severe, particularly regarding passport renewals and applications. While many taxpayers may perceive tax issues as purely financial, the reality is that the IRS, under the Fixing America's Surface Transportation (FAST) Act, has been increasingly using travel restrictions to enforce tax compliance. This Act allows the IRS to certify taxpayers with seriously delinquent tax debt to the U.S. Department of State, potentially leading to the denial of a passport application, the rejection of a renewal, or even the revocation of an existing passport.

The FAST Act, a powerful tool in the hands of the IRS, is designed to target individuals with unresolved tax debts, particularly those who owe more than $55,000 in unpaid taxes, penalties, and interest. If the IRS certifies your tax debt as seriously delinquent, the U.S. Department of State will be notified, and your passport privileges may be suspended or denied. This is not just a minor inconvenience; it can disrupt the lives of business professionals, expatriates, or even those planning a family vacation who suddenly find their travel plans in disarray due to a denied passport.[73]

Now, we will address the concerns of passport issues due to tax debt, offering practical guidance for resolution. As a tax expert, I have assisted numerous clients caught off guard by passport denials from delinquent taxes. I aim to help you comprehend the legal framework of these issues and, more importantly, equip you with actionable steps to regain control of

---

[73] https://www.irs.gov/newsroom/individuals-with-significant-tax-debt-should-act-promptly-to-avoid-revocation-of-passports

your financial situation and restore your freedom to travel. You are not alone in this; I am here to guide you.

This chapter will delve into the critical aspects of how the FAST Act affects taxpayers, what constitutes "seriously delinquent" tax debt, and what steps you can take if you find yourself in this situation. You will also find real-world examples of individuals who successfully overcame these challenges with the right strategy, underscoring the importance of timely action and professional help. Remember, the key to resolving these issues is acting promptly. By the end of this chapter, you will clearly understand how to shield yourself from travel restrictions due to tax non-compliance and, if necessary, how to resolve these issues with the IRS effectively.

The FAST Act and IRS Authority

The Fixing America's Surface Transportation (FAST) Act, signed into law in December 2015, is primarily known for its focus on highway funding and infrastructure improvements. However, hidden within this legislation is a consequential provision that directly impacts taxpayers with unresolved IRS debts. This provision grants the IRS the authority to certify individuals with "seriously delinquent" tax debt to the U.S. Department of State, effectively allowing the government to deny or revoke passports for those who owe significant taxes. As a tax expert, I've seen this act come into play many times, often catching individuals off-guard who had no idea their tax issues could affect something as fundamental as international travel.

Definition and Purpose of the FAST Act

While the FAST Act's primary purpose was to secure funding for transportation-related projects, a critical part of this law was designed to address the tax collection issue. The IRS's power to work with the State Department to deny or revoke passports for seriously delinquent taxpayers is a significant enforcement tool. It ensures that taxpayers who are not meeting their obligations cannot continue to ignore their debts without facing severe consequences, including losing access to international travel. The Act provides a mechanism for the IRS to incentivize taxpayers further to resolve their obligations, and it has become an effective strategy in debt collection.

How the IRS Certifies Seriously Delinquent Tax Debt

To understand the impact of the FAST Act, it is crucial to know how the IRS defines "seriously delinquent" tax debt. According to the IRS, a taxpayer's debt is considered seriously delinquent if it exceeds $55,000, including interest and penalties, and if the IRS has issued a Notice of Federal Tax Lien or a levy. Once this threshold is met, the IRS can certify the taxpayer's debt to the U.S. Department of State. This certification can trigger immediate consequences, such as denying a passport application or renewal.[74]

Consequences of IRS Certification

The certification process has several profound implications for individuals looking to travel internationally. The U.S. Department of State will not issue or renew your passport if the IRS certifies you as having seriously delinquent tax debt. In extreme cases, individuals possessing a valid visa may have it revoked or denied if they attempt to use it for travel. This can result in severe disruptions to personal and professional plans, particularly for individuals whose livelihoods depend on international travel.

---

[74] https://www.irs.gov/businesses/small-businesses-self-employed/revocation-or-denial-of-passport-in-cases-of-certain-unpaid-taxes

Let's break down the specific consequences of IRS certification:

1. **Passport Application Denial**: If you apply for a passport and the IRS has certified your tax debt, your application will be denied. This can prevent you from taking a business trip, vacation, or attending an important family event overseas.
2. **Passport Renewal Denial**: If you attempt to renew your passport while carrying a seriously delinquent tax debt, the State Department will deny your renewal request, limiting travel opportunities.
3. **Seizure of Current Passports**: In some cases, existing passports can be seized if the individual attempts to travel internationally while flagged by the IRS. This is particularly problematic if someone is abroad and unaware of their tax situation.

Driver's License Suspension Due to Unpaid Taxes: Procedures and Solutions

In some states, unpaid taxes can lead to your driver's license suspension or revocation. This measure is implemented to encourage taxpayers to settle their debts. For instance, in New York, if you owe $10,000 or more in back taxes, the state can recommend the suspension of your driver's license.

You will receive a Notice of Proposed Driver's License Suspension and have 60 days to resolve your tax debt. You can pay the debt in full or set up an installment payment agreement to avoid suspension. Certain exemptions, such as holding a commercial driver's license or receiving public assistance benefits, may apply. It's crucial to act promptly and communicate with the tax authorities to manage your debt and prevent further penalties.

Intervention by Tax Professionals

This is where tax professionals play a critical role. Tax professionals can assist with the resolution process when a taxpayer faces passport issues due to unresolved tax debt. Professionals can facilitate the decertification of their clients' debt by helping taxpayers file overdue returns, negotiate installment agreements, or qualify for other tax relief options, such as an Offer in Compromise (OIC).[75] This decertification lifts the travel restrictions, allowing individuals to move forward with their travel plans once the debt is either paid off or resolved through IRS-approved channels.

Case Study 1: James' Passport Application Denial

James, an international consultant, relied heavily on his ability to travel abroad for business. However, when he applied for a new passport, he received a denial from the State Department. Upon further investigation, we discovered that James had several years of unfiled tax returns and a substantial amount of tax debt that exceeded $60,000. The IRS had certified him as having seriously delinquent tax debt, so his passport application was denied.

The Reason for Denial

James had unknowingly allowed his tax situation to spiral out of control. Over the years, his failure to file returns and address his growing tax liability had resulted in mounting penalties and interest. Eventually, the debt crossed the threshold for serious delinquency under the FAST Act, and the IRS issued a certification to the Department of State. As a result, James found himself unable to obtain a passport at a time when his business required urgent international travel.

---

[75] https://scltaxlaw.com/irs-passport-restrictions/

Steps Taken to Resolve the Issue

The first step in resolving James' issue was addressing his unfiled tax returns. As his tax representative, I worked with him to gather all necessary documents, including W-2s and 1099s from past years. We prepared and submitted the missing returns, which allowed us to begin negotiating with the IRS. Once his returns were filed, the next phase was setting up a manageable payment plan for his outstanding debt. James' substantial tax debt made him eligible for an installment agreement, which we negotiated with the IRS on his behalf.

Outcome

With his returns filed and an installment agreement in place, we were able to work with the IRS to decertify James' seriously delinquent tax debt. Once the IRS notified the State Department of this decertification, James could finally reapply for his passport, which was approved without issue. This case highlights the importance of timely tax filing and addressing tax debts before they escalate to affect one's ability to travel.

Expert Commentary

James' case perfectly shows how tax issues can compound if not handled promptly. A few unfiled tax returns eventually led to a significant travel disruption. The key takeaway is that proactive tax management, including filing and responding to IRS notices promptly, can prevent situations like James'. For those already facing passport denials due to tax debts, the best course of action is to work with a tax professional who can guide you through resolving your tax issues and restoring your travel rights.

Passport Renewal Rejections Due to Tax Debt

One of the most surprising ways unresolved tax debts can disrupt your life is through passport renewal denials. Many individuals approach their passport renewals expecting it to be a simple, routine process, only to find that their application has been denied due to outstanding tax issues. This mainly concerns individuals who rely on international travel for work or those with personal commitments abroad. As a tax professional, I have seen firsthand how seriously delinquent tax debt can halt these renewals and the consequences it can have on a taxpayer's life.[76]

Under the FAST Act, once your tax debt exceeds $55,000, including interest and penalties, and you have received a Notice of Federal Tax Lien or a levy, the IRS can certify this debt to the U.S. Department of State. Once this certification is made, your passport renewal will be automatically rejected. The State Department's actions are swift and decisive in these cases, leaving individuals in a precarious situation if they need to travel for any reason.

Case Study of Nicole

Let me share the case of Nicole, a successful entrepreneur planning to renew her passport for an upcoming business trip. Nicole had always been diligent in running her company, but in her financial matters, she had allowed her tax filings to fall behind. Unbeknownst to her, she had accumulated a substantial tax debt over the years due to unfiled returns and unpaid taxes. It was only when she submitted her passport renewal application and received a denial letter from the Department of State that she realized the gravity of her situation.

Nicole was shocked by the denial. She had no idea that her unresolved tax issues could interfere with her ability to travel. Upon contacting me, we quickly identified the problem: her missing tax returns resulted in unpaid debt exceeding the "seriously delinquent" status threshold. The IRS had certified her

---

[76] https://travel.state.gov/content/travel/en/passports/legal-matters/passports-and-seriously-delinquent-tax-debt.html

debt to the State Department, triggering the rejection of her passport renewal.

The solution was clear. We needed to file Nicole's overdue tax returns immediately and begin settling her outstanding debt with the IRS. The first step was to gather her financial records and reconstruct the missing years' tax returns. Once we filed the returns, it became apparent that she owed a significant amount of taxes. However, because Nicole was willing to take swift action, we negotiated a payment plan with the IRS that allowed her to begin resolving her debt.

With the returns filed and a payment agreement in place, we contacted the IRS to request that they decertify her seriously delinquent status. After a brief negotiation and documentation review, the IRS lifted the certification, and Nicole could renew her passport in time for her business trip.

Commentary on the Urgency of Addressing Tax Debts Before Renewal

Nicole's experience highlights an important lesson for all taxpayers: unresolved tax debt doesn't just affect your finances; it can severely limit your ability to travel. The IRS and State Department's coordination under the FAST Act is designed to incentivize taxpayers to resolve their debts, and the consequences for ignoring these obligations can be immediate and far-reaching. The urgency of addressing tax debts before attempting to renew your passport cannot be overstated.

If you know that your tax filings are not up-to-date or that you owe a significant amount of back taxes, it is critical to resolve these issues as soon as possible. The process of filing returns and settling debts can take time, and the sooner you begin, the better your chances of avoiding a passport denial or revocation.[77]

---

[77] https://www.jdavidtaxlaw.com/irs-passport-revocation-or-denial/

Working with a tax professional can streamline this process, ensuring that your filings are accurate and that you have a solid plan for resolving any outstanding tax liabilities. By staying proactive, you can prevent tax debt from interfering with your travel plans and maintain control over your financial situation.

Case Study 2: Marina's Airport Incident and Passport Seizure

Marina's situation is one that no traveler expects but is a stark reminder of the consequences of unresolved tax debt. Marina, a business executive, was on her way to an essential overseas meeting when she was stopped at the airport. Upon checking in for her flight, she was informed that her passport had been flagged and was no longer valid for travel. Confused and frustrated, Marina learned that her passport had been seized due to delinquent tax debt certified by the IRS under the FAST Act.

This situation arose because Marina had accumulated a substantial tax debt that exceeded the $55,000 threshold set by the IRS for "seriously delinquent" tax debt. The FAST Act allows the IRS to notify the Department of State when a taxpayer reaches this threshold, leading to passport denial or seizure. In Marina's case, her failure to address several years of unfiled tax returns and unpaid taxes resulted in this drastic measure.

Steps for Immediate Resolution

When Marina reached out for help, it was clear that immediate action was needed. The first step was to address her unfiled tax returns. We quickly gathered the necessary financial documentation and filed the overdue returns. This step alone showed the IRS that she took her tax obligations seriously. Negotiating with the IRS for relief would not have been possible without filing these returns.

Once the returns were filed, we negotiated with the IRS to set up a partial payment arrangement. Given Marina's substantial tax debt, paying it in full was not feasible in the short term. However, the IRS allows for partial payments if the taxpayer is willing to enter into a structured payment plan.[78] We initiated a payment agreement that satisfied the IRS's requirements by demonstrating that Marina was willing to make payments based on her financial capacity.

The final step was to work with the IRS to decertify Marina's seriously delinquent status. Once her payment plan was in place, we petitioned the IRS to inform the Department of State that Marina's tax debt was no longer classified as delinquent. This process allowed her passport to be released, and she could reschedule her trip.

Expert Advice: How to Avoid Such Extreme Cases

Marina's case illustrates the importance of staying on top of your tax obligations, particularly if you travel internationally. To avoid facing such extreme measures, I advise all taxpayers to ensure that they remain compliant with tax filings and payments. If you are behind on taxes, the key is to act quickly. Ignoring IRS notices or delaying the filing of returns will only make matters worse. A proactive approach, which includes regular filings and timely payments or agreeing with the IRS, can prevent your passport from being flagged or seized. And, of course, working with a tax professional can streamline the process and ensure you avoid costly mistakes.

IRS Installment Agreements and Passport Certification Lifting

IRS installment agreements can be a lifeline for individuals facing significant tax debt, particularly when delinquent taxes threaten to interfere with passport applications or renewals. An IRS installment agreement is a payment plan allowing taxpayers

---

[78] https://gordonlaw.com/irs-notice-cp508c/

to settle their outstanding debt over time rather than in a lump sum. This option is critical for many taxpayers to manage significant tax liabilities without immediate collection actions like levies or passport restrictions.

What They Are and How They Work

An installment agreement is a formal arrangement with the IRS that allows taxpayers to pay their tax debt in manageable monthly payments over a set period. This can be particularly useful for taxpayers who owe more than they can immediately afford to pay but are willing to commit to paying off their debt gradually. The IRS typically offers different installment agreements based on the amount owed and the taxpayer's financial situation, including streamlined agreements for smaller debts and partial payment agreements for larger, more complicated cases.[79]

The process begins with filing all required tax returns—something the IRS will not negotiate on. Once tax compliance is established, the taxpayer can apply for an installment agreement, typically by submitting IRS Form 9465 (Installment Agreement Request) and financial information. The IRS will review the taxpayer's ability to pay, and if approved, the taxpayer can begin making monthly payments. The benefit of an installment agreement is that it can stop IRS collection efforts, including passport denials and revocations, as long as the taxpayer complies with the agreement.

Case Study of Lester

Lester's story perfectly illustrates how an installment agreement can lift passport-related restrictions. Lester, a retired engineer, found himself in a difficult situation when he attempted to renew his passport. He had accumulated over $70,000 in tax

---

[79] https://aliziolaw.com/irs-passport-revocation-cp508c/

debt due to unfiled returns and unpaid taxes from previous years. Like many taxpayers, Lester hadn't realized that his tax debt had grown to the point where it would affect his ability to renew his passport. When his renewal application was denied, he contacted me for assistance.

The first step was to file Lester's overdue tax returns. Without being current on all filings, the IRS would not consider installment agreements or other resolutions. After filing the returns, we worked closely with Lester to assess his financial situation. Given his fixed retirement income, it was clear that paying off the entire debt in one lump sum was not feasible. However, the IRS offers installment agreements specifically designed for individuals who cannot afford to pay their tax debt in full but can make regular payments over time.

We submitted a request for a streamlined installment agreement, which is available to taxpayers owing less than $50,000. Since Lester's debt exceeded this amount, we also provided additional financial information to support the request. Once the agreement was approved, Lester began making monthly payments, which fit comfortably within his budget.

Certification Lifting and Successful Passport Renewal

With the installment agreement in place, the next step was to address the issue of Lester's passport renewal. Because Lester was now in compliance with his tax filings and had established a payment plan, we requested that the IRS decertify his seriously delinquent tax status. This process typically involves contacting the IRS and providing proof of the installment agreement; at this point, the IRS notifies the Department of State that the taxpayer is no longer considered seriously delinquent. Once the decertification was processed, Lester could renew his passport successfully.

Expert Insight: Why Installment Agreements Are a Key Tool

Installment agreements are among the most effective tools available for taxpayers facing significant tax debt, particularly those at risk of passport denial or revocation. They allow taxpayers to resolve their debt manageable and provide a pathway to decertify seriously delinquent status, thereby restoring passport privileges. An installment agreement offers a viable solution to tax and travel concerns for individuals like Lester, who require a passport for personal or professional reasons.

However, it is essential to remember that the IRS will require full compliance with the terms of the agreement. Missing a payment or failing to file future returns on time can result in the reinstatement of seriously delinquent status, putting your passport and financial stability at risk again.[80] For these reasons, working with a tax professional who can help structure the agreement and ensure compliance is crucial to maintaining your travel privileges and managing your tax debt effectively.

Legal and Practical Considerations

When faced with denying or seizing a passport due to tax debt, taxpayers must understand their legal rights and the steps they can take to resolve the situation. The FAST Act empowers the IRS to restrict passport issuance for those with "seriously delinquent" tax debt, but it does not mean that affected individuals are without options. As a tax professional, many taxpayers panic when confronted with a passport denial. Still, realizing that this serious situation is not without remedies is essential.

[80] https://www.gartzmantaxlaw.com/blog/2019/11/how-to-request-a-reversal-of-irs-passport-actions/

Legal Rights of Taxpayers Facing Passport Denial or Seizure

First and foremost, taxpayers have the right to be informed. If the IRS certifies your tax debt to the U.S. Department of State, you will receive a notification (Notice CP508C) from the IRS outlining the certification. This notice is a critical document, as it serves as the first official indication that your travel privileges are at risk. You also have the right to appeal if you believe the certification was made in error. For example, if you are already in an installment agreement or have filed an Offer in Compromise (OIC), the IRS is not supposed to certify your debt. In such cases, taxpayers can file an appeal using IRS Form 911, requesting assistance from the Taxpayer Advocate Service.

Important Deadlines and the Urgency of Addressing IRS Notices

When dealing with passport issues due to tax debt, time is of the essence. IRS notices come with deadlines; failure to act within those timelines can make the situation more difficult to resolve. For example, once your debt is certified as seriously delinquent, the Department of State will hold your passport application or renewal until the certification is resolved. If planning international travel, you must act quickly to avoid disruptions.

Ignoring IRS notices or delaying filing overdue returns can significantly worsen your situation. In my experience, the sooner taxpayers address the IRS certifications and notices, the better their chances of resolving the issue without facing more severe consequences such as levies, liens, or legal actions. It is always best to approach IRS notices urgently, as the window for preventing further complications is often short.

Role of Tax Professionals in Resolving Passport-Related Issues

Resolving passport issues related to tax debt often requires professional intervention, as the process can be complex and time-sensitive. Here's how tax professionals can assist:

- **Negotiating with the IRS**: A skilled tax professional can negotiate with the IRS to resolve your tax debt, preventing or lifting the certification of delinquent debt. Whether through installment agreements, Offers in Compromise, or other resolutions, a tax expert knows the ins and outs of these negotiations and can significantly increase the likelihood of a favorable outcome.
- **Filing Overdue Returns**: One of the most common reasons for passport denials is unfiled tax returns. Tax professionals can help you file these returns promptly, ensuring compliance and setting the stage for negotiations with the IRS. They can also assist in gathering necessary documents, such as W-2s or 1099s if you're missing any records.[81]
- **Navigating Installment Agreements or Offers in Compromise (OIC)**: An installment agreement or an OIC may be the best option for taxpayers who cannot pay their total tax debt upfront. Tax professionals can help determine which option is more appropriate based on your financial situation. An installment agreement allows you to make monthly payments, while an OIC lets you settle your debt for less than the total amount owed. Both options can lead to the decertification of your debt and the restoration of your passport privileges.

---

[81] https://www.irs.gov/irm/part5/irm_05-019-025

Preventing Passport Issues by Staying Compliant

The best way to avoid passport-related issues is to comply with IRS filing and payment requirements. Filing your tax returns on time, paying any taxes due, or entering into an agreement if you cannot pay will prevent the IRS from certifying your debt. If you are behind on taxes, take immediate action to resolve the situation. Working with a tax professional ensures that you remain compliant and avoid the pitfalls of non-compliance, such as passport denial or seizure. Prevention is always more effective—and less stressful—than scrambling to resolve a crisis at the last minute.

Case Study: International Travel and Tax Compliance

Marina's situation is an unfortunate but typical example of how unresolved tax debt can disrupt international travel. Marina, a global consultant, had planned a business trip overseas when she was unexpectedly stopped at the airport. She was informed that her passport was no longer valid due to tax debt, leaving her stranded at the airport and unable to travel. Understandably, Marina was shocked, as she hadn't realized her tax debt could result in severe consequences.

IRS Process of Passport Certification and How It Affects International Travel

Marina's case fell under the provisions of the FAST Act, which allows the IRS to certify taxpayers with "seriously delinquent" tax debt. In Marina's case, her unpaid taxes and penalties had accumulated over $55,000, triggering the IRS certification. Once the IRS notified the Department of State, Marina's passport was effectively revoked, preventing her from leaving the country for her business trip.

Expert Intervention

When Marina contacted me, the first step was to address her overdue tax returns. We quickly gathered all necessary documentation and filed her missing returns, which was the root cause of her accumulating penalties. Filing these returns was the essential first step, as the IRS would not consider negotiating her tax debt without compliance.

After filing her returns, we negotiated with the IRS to set up a partial payment arrangement. Given Marina's financial situation, paying the entire amount at once was not feasible, but by setting up a structured payment plan, we demonstrated her willingness to resolve the debt. Once the IRS accepted this payment arrangement, they decertified her seriously delinquent status.

Results

With her debt no longer classified as seriously delinquent, Marina's passport certification was lifted. She was able to reapply for a passport and continue her international travel. This case highlights how quickly a professional intervention can turn things around when dealing with passport issues related to tax debt.

Impacts of Tax Non-Compliance on International Mobility

Marina's experience demonstrates the impact tax non-compliance can have on international travel. It is not just about owing money to the IRS: it is about how unresolved debt can interfere with essential parts of your life, such as traveling for work or personal reasons. The IRS's power to certify delinquent debt and restrict travel is a potent tool, but timely professional intervention can resolve these situations efficiently.[82]

Throughout this chapter, we've explored how unresolved tax debts can lead to severe consequences under the FAST Act, specifically regarding passport applications, renewals, and revocations. The FAST Act grants the IRS the authority to certify seriously delinquent tax debt to the U.S. Department of State, and this certification can result in the denial or seizure of your passport. This can be a disruptive and stressful situation for those who rely on international travel—whether for business, personal reasons, or emergencies.

We've seen through various case studies, such as those of James, Nicole, and Marina, how unresolved tax debts can directly interfere with one's ability to travel. Each case demonstrated the severe consequences of ignoring tax filings or delaying payment of overdue taxes. However, these stories also highlighted how these issues can be resolved with the right approach and the help of a qualified tax professional. Filing overdue tax returns, negotiating payment agreements, and working with the IRS to decertify seriously delinquent status are all viable solutions that can restore your passport privileges and give you peace of mind.

The role of tax professionals in resolving these issues cannot be overstated. Whether negotiating an installment agreement, filing missing returns, or settling your debt through an Offer in Compromise (OIC), tax professionals have the knowledge and experience to guide you through the complexities of IRS regulations. Their intervention can prevent travel disruptions and help you regain control over your financial situation.[83]

---

[82] https://www.plunkettcooney.com/dontbetthebusinessblog/IRS-passport-program
[83] https://gallerosrobinson.com/insight-inside/irs-tax-debt-could-affect-passport-renewal/

Staying compliant with tax laws is the best way to avoid passport-related complications. Filing timely returns and promptly addressing any tax debt can prevent the IRS from certifying your debt to the Department of State. If you face passport issues due to unresolved tax debt, I strongly encourage you to seek professional help. Resolving these matters with expert assistance not only protects your travel rights but also ensures that you avoid further financial consequences in the future. Taking action sooner rather than later is the key to maintaining economic stability and the freedom to travel without restriction.

Chapter 11: Stress and Anxiety

As a tax professional, I've witnessed the profound impact that non-compliance with tax obligations, particularly unfiled tax returns, can have on a person's mental health. This is a theoretical issue that I've seen affect real people. While most tax discussions focus on financial consequences, it's crucial to recognize the significant emotional toll that non-compliance can impose. Unfiled tax returns are not just an administrative oversight; they often weigh heavily on the mental well-being of those affected.

Let's be clear: failing to file tax returns can create an overwhelming sense of dread. For many, the thought of what may come from the IRS looms large. There's often a misconception that tax-related anxiety is limited to financial strain, but the emotional impact runs much more profound.[84] People experience sleepless nights, persistent worry, and, in some cases, feelings of hopelessness. These emotional responses are not unfounded. The fear of penalties, back taxes, and even the potential for legal action can escalate a situation that feels unmanageable.

But there is a growing recognition, even within the financial services industry, of the link between mental health and economic well-being. Tax-related stress can intensify, especially when it involves long-standing tax issues that have been ignored or postponed. People can feel trapped, burdened by their tax obligations, yet uncertain about where to begin. The emotional weight of these situations often leads to avoidance, which only worsens matters. The longer the delay, the more the financial and emotional burdens grow.

Consider this: a missed tax filing can snowball into years of financial uncertainty and anxiety. Even when people can meet

---

[84] https://www.myirstaxrelief.com/back-tax-help/when-to-call-a-tax-relief-service/tax-iety-tax-anxiety-stress/

their obligations, the psychological impact of unresolved tax issues can lead them to procrastinate. The mere thought of confronting their tax situation can paralyze them, reinforcing the cycle of anxiety and avoidance. However, it's important to remember that what began as a minor oversight can be resolved with the proper support and guidance, offering a significant source of emotional relief.[85]

As a tax professional, I understand this cycle all too well, so I encourage my clients to address these issues as soon as possible. It will alleviate the financial strain, but taking proactive steps can bring immense emotional relief. My job is not just to resolve economic problems; it helps my clients find peace of mind. Financial and emotional burdens are intricately linked, and determining one often alleviates the other.

Tax professionals can and should be seen as a financial and emotional support source. By assisting in the timely and accurate filing of tax returns, we can provide individuals with the clarity and guidance needed to reduce their anxiety. Remember, addressing your tax issues doesn't just improve your financial standing; it contributes significantly to your overall well-being.

Understanding Tax-Related Stress and Anxiety

The emotional strain caused by unresolved tax obligations, particularly unfiled returns, is more common than many realize. When someone fails to meet their tax requirements, it often triggers a cascade of mental health challenges. Stress and anxiety are the most prevalent responses, but they can quickly escalate into more severe conditions such as depression or chronic emotional distress.

---

[85] https://www.irs.gov/newsroom/tips-to-help-taxpayers-reduce-tax-time-stress

From my professional experience, I've seen how unfiled tax returns can cause people to worry constantly. The uncertainty surrounding their tax liability, not knowing how much they owe or whether penalties are accruing, fuels anxiety. It's not just the financial burden; it's the overwhelming sense of not being in control of one's economic future. This loss of power is at the heart of much of the stress accompanying tax non-compliance.[86]

Research supports the idea that financial uncertainty can have a profound impact on mental health. Studies have shown that individuals dealing with financial stress, including tax-related issues, are more likely to experience anxiety, panic attacks, and feelings of helplessness. The looming threat of IRS action—whether through letters, penalties, or audits—compounds these feelings. Even for those who are financially stable, the fear of what might happen can be debilitating.

Take, for instance, the IRS's ability to impose penalties or initiate collection efforts. Many people have an inherent fear of the IRS, even if they've done nothing wrong. This fear is amplified for those who know they've neglected their tax filings. Every letter from the IRS or notification of interest and penalties adds to the stress. The potential legal ramifications, such as wage garnishments or liens, weigh heavily on individuals, making it difficult for them to focus on their day-to-day responsibilities.[87]

One of the most potent triggers for tax-related anxiety is the unknown. Individuals don't clearly understand how much they owe or what penalties have been applied without filing returns. This creates a state of financial limbo, leaving them vulnerable to growing stress. And the longer they wait to address these issues, the more severe the anxiety becomes. Many individuals describe

---

[86] https://www.calm.com/blog/tax-anxiety

[87] https://thestudentlawyer.com/2024/07/20/let-an-expert-tax-attorney-help-you-deal-with-irs-stress/

this as living with constant dread, always wondering when the other shoe will drop.

Most individuals are not familiar with the complexities of tax laws, which exacerbates the issue. They may feel overwhelmed by the prospect of tackling their tax debt, uncertain where to start, and worried that any action they take could worsen things. In my experience, this sense of helplessness often prevents people from seeking help sooner. Instead, they delay, hoping the problem will disappear independently. It never does.

As an expert in this field, I can confidently say that one of the best ways to alleviate this stress is to provide individuals with a clear, actionable plan. By helping people understand exactly where they stand with the IRS and outlining a step-by-step process for addressing their unfiled returns, we can reduce the anxiety that stems from the unknown. Having a plan restores a sense of control, which is critical for improving financial and mental well-being.

In my practice, I often see clients living with tax-related stress for years. Many of them tell me that they immediately feel relief once we begin filing their returns and working with the IRS. It's not just about reducing their financial liability; it's about knowing they're no longer in limbo. They're taking action, and that alone can significantly reduce their anxiety.

The most important takeaway for anyone dealing with tax-related stress is this: you're not alone, and there are solutions. By seeking professional help, you can alleviate the financial burden and the emotional toll of unresolved tax issues. Tax professionals like myself are here to guide you through the process, offering technical expertise and support to regain control of your financial life and mental health.[88]

Real-Life Examples of Tax-Induced Stress

In my practice, I've seen how unresolved tax obligations can wreak havoc on people's mental health, and it's not limited to their finances. The emotional and psychological toll is often immense, leading to sleepless nights, overwhelming stress, and even depression. Allow me to share a few real-life examples that illustrate the challenges individuals face when they delay filing their tax returns and how, through strategic intervention, we helped alleviate their financial burdens and mental strain.

Lilah's Case Study: A Freelance Writer's Struggle with Unfiled Taxes

Lilah, a successful freelance writer, came to me after enduring two years of sleepless nights. She was consumed by the fear of what might happen if the IRS discovered her unfiled tax returns. Her anxiety wasn't just financial; it was emotional and mental. She worried constantly about penalties, interest, and the looming possibility of legal action. Her tax situation began to overshadow her professional life, making it difficult for her to focus on her writing. The constant worry and guilt over her non-compliance became a heavy burden that weighed on her daily.

When Lilah finally sought my assistance, she was at her breaking point. We immediately got to work, organizing her financial documents and filing her overdue returns. More importantly, we developed a clear and manageable plan to handle the resulting tax liabilities. The impact was immediate. Lilah's relief was palpable as her sleepless nights became a thing of the past. Having a clear path forward reduced her anxiety

---

[88] https://www.cnbc.com/2024/04/01/gen-zers-say-theyll-need-a-therapist-to-deal-with-tax-filing-stress.html

significantly. Knowing that professionals handled her tax issues, she could return her focus to her career.

Terry's Case Study: Navigating Tax Stress in the Café Business

A small café owner, Terry, faced a different but equally challenging situation. His café had been growing steadily, but the mounting pressure of his unfiled tax returns began seeping into his business and personal life. He had no idea how much he owed the IRS, which caused him immense stress. The uncertainty of his tax obligations distracted him from the day-to-day operations of his café, affecting his decision-making and overall productivity.

When Terry came to me, he was overwhelmed. The stress had built up to a point where it affected his business and relationships. We immediately took control of the situation by organizing his financial records and filing the outstanding tax returns. Once we clarified his tax obligations, we negotiated a manageable payment plan with the IRS. The relief Terry felt was undeniable. With his tax situation under control, he could focus on what he loved: running his café without the constant cloud of uncertainty hanging over him.

Melony's Case Study: Navigating Tax Anxiety as a Single Mother

Perhaps one of the most heart-wrenching cases was Melony's. A single mother and small business owner, Melony had accumulated significant tax debt over several years. The weight of her tax burden became too much, and she fell into a deep depression, worrying about how she would manage her debt while providing for her family. Her tax situation felt like an insurmountable obstacle, which she believed would jeopardize her family's future.

When I began working with Melony, it was clear that her emotional state was tied closely to her financial problems. The first step was to tackle the unfiled returns and get a handle on her tax situation. We applied for an Offer in Compromise (OIC), which reduced her debt to a manageable level, and we established a realistic payment plan. The transformation was remarkable. With her tax issues under control, Melony began to feel hopeful again. Her depression lifted as she regained control over her financial situation and, more importantly, her life.

These examples demonstrate that tax non-compliance doesn't just affect your finances—it affects your mental well-being. But with the proper professional guidance, you can find relief from both the financial and emotional burden.

Role of Tax Professionals in Providing Emotional Support

As a tax professional, my role goes far beyond simply resolving financial issues. In many cases, the most significant impact on my clients is providing them with emotional support during highly stressful situations. Taxes, particularly unfiled returns, can be a source of immense anxiety, but with the proper guidance, that stress can be reduced dramatically.

One of the most essential services we offer is clarity. When facing unfiled returns or tax debt, the uncertainty surrounding their obligations can be paralyzing. They're often unsure what they owe, what penalties may be imposed, or whether legal action could follow. This lack of clarity leads to fear, which can quickly spiral into panic or avoidance. By providing a clear and actionable plan, we help clients regain control over their financial situation, and that control is critical to reducing stress.[89]

[89] https://www.webmd.com/balance/stress-management/features/cope-tax-time-stress

Take Lilah, the freelance writer, for instance. Her sleepless nights were driven by fear of the unknown—how much she owed, what penalties might be coming, and whether she was in legal jeopardy. We filed her overdue returns and negotiated a payment plan; she had a roadmap. That sense of direction reduced her anxiety almost immediately. The mental relief she experienced wasn't just a byproduct of resolving her tax debt. It was the direct result of knowing a plan was in place.

Tax professionals also provide emotional relief by handling the heavy lifting. For many clients, just interacting with the IRS is overwhelming. While not inherently adversarial, the IRS represents authority, and the fear of penalties or audits can induce significant stress. When we step in, we provide technical expertise and act as a buffer between the client and the IRS. This creates peace of mind, knowing that someone is advocating on their behalf and managing the situation.

Terry, the café owner, experienced this firsthand. The stress he felt wasn't just about owing money; it was about the uncertainty of the situation and the daunting prospect of dealing with the IRS. By stepping in, we could remove that burden from Terry's shoulders. He no longer had to worry about the details of his tax obligations because he knew we were handling them. This sense of relief allowed him to focus on his business, where his attention was needed.

Emotional support also comes from providing reassurance during the most challenging times. For Melony, the single mother facing depression, her tax debt felt like an insurmountable obstacle. However, by working with her to file her returns and negotiate an OIC, we not only reduced her debt but restored her sense of hope. This emotional turnaround was critical for her recovery, showing how tax professionals can provide more than financial solutions—they offer a lifeline during times of mental strain.

In essence, tax professionals are problem solvers. By resolving the financial problems that trigger stress and anxiety, we help restore emotional balance. The relief clients feel when they see a clear path forward and know their tax issues are being handled is palpable. It's not just about the numbers on paper; it's about providing peace of mind. And that, more than anything, is what makes our role so vital.

The Financial Stress Cycle

In my years of experience, I have seen how the uncertainty surrounding tax liabilities can create a destructive cycle of stress. When taxes remain unfiled, the anxiety and fear surrounding potential consequences grow, often leading to avoidance. Unfortunately, avoidance doesn't solve the problem—it makes it worse. This procrastination only increases the financial strain and exacerbates the mental burden, creating a self-perpetuating cycle that can feel impossible to escape.

Let's break down how this cycle works. It all starts with the initial decision—intentional or not—not to file taxes. For many, the problem begins with a seemingly minor issue: maybe they were unsure of how much they owed, or life events made it difficult to get their finances in order. Regardless of the reason, the decision to delay filing is usually the first step in a downward spiral.

Once the taxes are unfiled, the uncertainty begins to set in. People start wondering: How much do I owe? What penalties are accruing? Will the IRS come after me? This uncertainty breeds anxiety, and the longer it goes unaddressed, the more overwhelming the situation becomes. It's not uncommon for people to go months or years without filing simply because they feel paralyzed by the fear of what might happen.

One of my clients, Aaron, was caught in this exact cycle. He didn't file his taxes one year due to a family emergency, thinking he'd catch up the following year. But as time passed, the fear of penalties and legal action began to weigh on him. He procrastinated further, and the anxiety about his growing tax debt consumed him. Eventually, he stopped opening letters from the IRS altogether because the stress became too much to handle.

This kind of avoidance only prolongs the problem. As Aaron's case shows, each day that passes without filing leads to a greater sense of dread, which in turn leads to more avoidance. It's a vicious cycle, and the financial impact only worsens.[90] Interest and penalties accrue, making the situation feel even more insurmountable. The result? People become trapped in a state of inaction, feeling powerless to address the issues causing their stress.

As a tax professional, my role is to break that cycle. The first step is to help clients like Aaron confront their tax situation head-on. Once we sit down and begin organizing their financial records, the sense of relief is almost immediate. Filing those overdue returns, even if penalties are involved, gives people a clear picture of their obligations. It transforms the unknown into something concrete—something they can finally manage. And that's the key to reducing their mental strain.

By providing an actionable plan, we turn what once felt overwhelming into manageable steps. This restoration of control is critical in breaking the cycle of stress and procrastination. Knowing there's a way forward gives people the mental and emotional space to address their financial situation rather than running from it.

---

[90] https://www.psychologytoday.com/intl/blog/mental-wealth/202302/seven-tips-to-help-manage-income-tax-stress

Managing Tax Anxiety in Relationships

Financial stress, mainly when it involves unfiled taxes, doesn't just affect the individual. It can also strain personal relationships. In my work, I've seen how unresolved tax issues lead to tension between partners, often causing friction in otherwise healthy relationships. The stress of dealing with tax debt can create an environment of blame, resentment, and anxiety, mainly when both partners are unsure how to address the problem.

One such case is that of Nelly and her husband. They had accumulated a significant tax debt over several years due to unfiled returns, and the stress of not knowing how to handle the situation was causing significant issues in their marriage. Nelly wanted to address the problem head-on, but her husband preferred to wait and hoped it would somehow resolve itself. This difference in approach led to frequent arguments, with each blaming the other for their financial predicament.

This type of tension is not uncommon. When tax debt piles up, it often leads to disagreements over handling it. One partner may feel overwhelmed by financial pressure, while the other may focus more on avoiding the issue. This disconnect creates a cycle of stress within the relationship, with the unresolved tax debt as a constant source of conflict.[91]

As tax professionals, part of our job is to mediate these conversations. In Nelly and her husband's case, I sat down with them to explain their options clearly. By providing a structured step-by-step plan to file their overdue returns and negotiate a payment plan with the IRS, I was able to help them move forward as a team. Once they understood their financial situation and had a clear path forward, the tension in their marriage began to ease.

---

[91] https://www.goldburdmccone.com/blog/2024/02/the-emotional-impact-of-irs-audits-coping-with-financial-scrutiny/

The key in situations like this is communication. Tax professionals provide more than just financial solutions; we help couples communicate more effectively about their tax issues. We bring clarity to the situation, explaining the consequences of non-compliance and outlining the steps that need to be taken. This process reduces the financial burden and alleviates the relational strain by providing both partners with the same understanding of the problem and the solution.

When both individuals are on the same page, they can approach the issue as a united front rather than placing blame on one another. The anxiety from financial uncertainty is replaced by the confidence that comes with knowing exactly what needs to be done. By mediating these discussions, tax professionals can help restore harmony in relationships strained by tax-related stress.

In Nelly and her husband's case, resolving their tax debt was not just a financial win but a personal one. Working through their financial challenges together strengthened their marriage. This shows that the role of a tax professional isn't limited to numbers; it extends into the emotional and relational aspects of our client's lives as well. By providing clear solutions, we reduce the stress that comes from uncertainty, improving our client's financial health and relationships.

Tax-Related Fear of Financial Ruin

The fear of financial ruin is a natural and paralyzing concern for many individuals facing unfiled tax returns or accumulating tax debts. The implications of unresolved tax obligations can be severe, with individuals fearing the loss of their homes, savings, or other vital assets. This anxiety can lead to a state of mental distress that affects every aspect of a person's life, creating a cycle of fear and inaction.

Take, for instance, the case of Aaron. He was a hardworking individual who had always managed his finances reasonably well.

However, a series of unforeseen events, including medical emergencies and a job loss, led him to fall behind on his tax obligations. As unfiled returns piled up, Aaron's anxiety escalated into a constant fear of losing his home. He envisioned scenarios where the IRS might place a lien on his property or initiate aggressive collection actions that could lead to foreclosure. This fear consumed him, causing sleepless nights and an inability to focus on his work or family life.

The emotional toll of fearing financial ruin can be crippled. When individuals like Aaron become overwhelmed with worry about their economic future, they often find it challenging to take proactive steps to remedy their situation. Instead of seeking help, they may retreat into avoidance, compounding their problems and amplifying their fears. This cycle of anxiety can make the thought of addressing their tax issues feel insurmountable.[92]

However, timely intervention with the IRS can make a significant difference. In Aaron's case, when he finally reached out for professional help, we assessed his tax liabilities and organized a strategy to address them effectively. We filed his overdue tax returns, which clarified his financial situation and provided a clear understanding of what he owed. This proactive approach was pivotal in easing his anxiety.

By negotiating a manageable payment plan with the IRS, we were able to protect Aaron's home from the threat of liens or other aggressive collection actions. Knowing that his property was safe significantly alleviated his fears. Rather than feeling trapped by his tax debt, Aaron had a structured path forward that empowered him to regain control over his financial situation.

---

[92] https://www.accountantsinmiami.com/tax-services/irs-representation-3.html?srsltid=AfmBOorMAu1l5mWYp9M_BUeMpwcp4FGCDE599ajoJJg6kztMGzjv1N7-

The lesson here is clear: timely intervention can protect valuable assets and significantly reduce anxiety around financial ruin. Working with a tax professional can clarify your obligations and provide the tools to navigate your tax challenges effectively. When individuals take that crucial step to confront their tax issues, they safeguard their financial future and pave the way for improved mental well-being.[93]

The Link between Mental Health and Financial Stability

It is essential to recognize that stress and anxiety are not merely byproducts of non-compliance with tax obligations—they are integral aspects of the financial landscape that many individuals navigate. The emotional burden of unresolved tax issues can weigh heavily on one's mental health, creating a vicious cycle of avoidance and escalating fears.

Throughout this chapter, I have highlighted various cases, including individuals like Aaron, Lilah, and Melony, who faced significant mental strain due to their tax situations. These stories illustrate the profound connection between financial challenges and mental health. It is not enough to address the numbers; we must also acknowledge the human aspect of tax compliance.

Tax professionals play a crucial role in this dynamic. We are not only here to resolve financial issues; we are also equipped to help restore mental well-being. Clear strategies and actionable plans empower individuals to confront their tax obligations head-on. This proactive approach alleviates the emotional burden of uncertainty and fosters a sense of control and stability in our clients' lives.

---

[93] https://highlandtaxresolution.com/uncategorized/dealing-with-the-frustration-and-anxiety-of-an-irs-mess/

Furthermore, I urge readers to take a proactive stance in managing their tax obligations. Delaying action can lead to heightened stress and a deeper entrenchment in financial difficulties. By seeking professional help early, individuals can safeguard not only their financial health but also their mental well-being.

Ultimately, the goal is to create a balanced financial management approach prioritizing fiscal responsibility and mental health. Remember, you are not alone in this journey. Seeking assistance from a qualified tax professional can be the first step towards reclaiming your peace of mind and ensuring a secure financial future. Together, we can break the cycle of stress and anxiety, paving the way for a healthier, more stable life.

Chapter 12: How Can You Overcome It All?

The Path to Tax Relief

Dealing with tax debt is an overwhelming experience for many. As someone who has guided countless individuals through the maze of tax regulations, I can tell you firsthand that facing a substantial tax bill is a challenge that affects more than just your bank account. It can impact your peace of mind, credit score, and ability to meet day-to-day financial obligations. However, it's important to remember that you're not alone, and the IRS provides several solutions to help taxpayers manage their debts more effectively.

I'll focus on two of the most commonly used tools for taxpayers seeking relief from overwhelming tax debt: Installment Agreements (IAs) and Offers in Compromise (OIC). These programs provide structured ways for individuals to address their tax liabilities without resorting to drastic measures like bankruptcy or risking collection actions such as wage garnishment or property liens.

We'll begin with Installment Agreements, a widely used solution that allows taxpayers to break down their debt into manageable monthly payments. This option benefits those who can't pay their entire tax bill upfront. I'll walk you through the different installment agreements available and show you how to choose the one that best fits your financial situation.

Next, we'll explore Offers in Compromise, a less common but precious option for individuals who cannot fully pay their tax debt due to severe financial hardship. Through the OIC program, the IRS may agree to settle your tax liability for less than the total amount owed, something that could be a game-changer if paying your entire debt is impossible.[94]

As with any financial decision, these options come with their own sets of rules, eligibility criteria, and potential risks. It's critical to understand that while these programs are designed to offer relief, they also require a clear understanding of your finances and the ability to meet the terms laid out by the IRS. Choosing the right option depends on several factors: income, assets, expenses, and overall ability to pay.

This is where the guidance of a tax professional can prove invaluable. Tax professionals bring specialized knowledge and years of experience navigating IRS processes, ensuring that you're fully compliant with all requirements while maximizing the benefits of these programs. Throughout this chapter, I'll highlight real-world examples of professional support distinguishing between financial recovery and ongoing hardship.

Understanding your options is the first step in overcoming tax issues. Whether you're considering an Installment Agreement or an Offer in Compromise, this chapter will provide the knowledge needed to make informed decisions about managing your tax debt. By the end, you'll clearly understand how to move forward with a plan that fits your unique situation and helps you regain control of your finances.

Understanding Installment Agreements (IAs)

When faced with the daunting task of paying off a significant tax debt, it's essential to understand that options are available to help you manage your financial obligations without overwhelming your day-to-day finances. One such option is the Installment Agreement (IA), a payment plan provided by the IRS, which allows taxpayers like you to break down their tax debt into

[94] https://howardlevyirslawyer.com/articles/

manageable monthly payments. In this section, I will walk you through what an Installment Agreement is, the types available, the process of applying for one, and the potential benefits and risks.

What is an Installment Agreement?

An Installment Agreement is a structured payment plan the IRS offers to taxpayers who cannot fully pay their tax debt by the due date. This agreement provides relief by allowing you to pay off your outstanding balance over some time rather than all at once, making it far easier to manage financially.[95] By opting for an IA, you avoid the immediate financial pressure and spread your payments over months or even years, depending on the type of agreement you qualify for.

The purpose of an Installment Agreement is straightforward: it enables taxpayers to remain in compliance with the IRS without risking collection actions such as liens or levies, which can severely affect your financial standing. Breaking down large debts into smaller, more manageable payments makes it easier to keep up with your obligations and helps prevent further penalties or actions from the IRS as long as you stay on track.

Types of Installment Agreements

The IRS doesn't offer a one-size-fits-all solution. There are various types of Installment Agreements designed to accommodate the specific financial situations of different taxpayers. Each type has its criteria, and understanding which one best suits your financial condition is critical to managing your debt effectively.

[95] https://www.wolfandco.com/national-cpa-firm/?utm_source=google&utm_medium=cpc&utm_campaign=general_brand&gclid=CjwKCAiAxKy5BhBbEiwAYiW--y-z5jEO8P6S4mH0fBqE-RHL1NIEiRQamBTWZJOlOKbSE7zg4ahb6hoCQi0QAvD_BwE

Guaranteed Installment Agreement

A Guaranteed Installment Agreement is available to taxpayers who owe $10,000 or less in taxes. If you've filed all required tax returns, haven't entered into another Installment Agreement within the last five years, and agree to pay off your debt within three years, the IRS will automatically approve this agreement. This option is highly structured, with little room for negotiation, but provides certainty for those with relatively small debts.

Streamlined Installment Agreement

Streamlined Installment Agreements are designed for taxpayers who owe up to $50,000. The benefit of this type is that it doesn't require submitting detailed financial documentation, which simplifies the process considerably. You can generally spread the payments over 72 months, provided you can meet the monthly payment requirements. This is the easiest and most efficient way for many to handle mid-range tax debt.

Partial Payment Installment Agreement (PPIA)

A PPIA is a more flexible option for those who cannot afford to pay the total amount they owe, even over time. With this arrangement, you'll pay what you can, and after a certain period, the remaining balance may be forgiven. However, securing this agreement is more complicated, as it requires a thorough review of your financial situation, including income, expenses, and asset equity. If you face significant economic hardship, it's a viable option, but be prepared for a more rigorous application process.

Non-Streamlined Installment Agreement

This option is available to those who owe over $50,000 or need a repayment period longer than 72 months. Since it doesn't follow the streamlined process, you'll need to provide detailed financial documentation, and the IRS will scrutinize your ability to pay. Non-streamlined agreements offer more repayment flexibility but have additional oversight and approval requirements. This type may be best if your debt exceeds the threshold for other contracts or your financial situation is particularly complex.

Application Process for IAs

Applying for an Installment Agreement is a structured process, but it's crucial to approach it with care. The IRS expects accuracy and completeness in your application, and providing thorough documentation is essential for approval.

To begin the process, you must submit **Form 9465 (Installment Agreement Request)**, which provides the IRS with basic information about your tax debt and your ability to make monthly payments. If your debt exceeds $50,000, or if you're applying for a non-streamlined or partial payment plan, you must also submit **Form 433-F (Collection Information Statement)**.[96] This form is where you disclose detailed information about your finances (income, expenses, and assets), which the IRS will use to evaluate your ability to pay.

Before applying, it's essential to assess your eligibility. Are you up to date with filing all your tax returns? Have you calculated an affordable monthly payment that you can sustain over time? These are critical steps that can determine whether your application is approved.

Once your application is submitted, the IRS will review your financial information and approve or deny the request. If

---

[96] https://wtaxgroup.co/lp/forgiveness.html?utm_campaign=irs-for&utm_term=need%20help%20with%20irs&gad_source=1&gclid=CjwKCAiAxKy5BhBbEiwAYiW--w2EBkGL7Xwovhsz1qK8ZcUrz1-wjm2JJNW3-Y_wjyph9E0Lc2KxbhoCs0wQAvD_BwE

approved, you'll receive a confirmation outlining the terms of the agreement, including the payment amount and due dates.

Benefits and Risks of Installment Agreements

Entering an Installment Agreement can be a wise decision, but it's not without its trade-offs. Let's explore both the benefits and risks.

- Benefits:
- Avoid Immediate Financial Strain: One of the most significant advantages of an Installment Agreement is that it simultaneously alleviates the pressure of paying off a large sum. By spreading your payments over time, you can maintain financial stability while gradually resolving your tax debt.
- Prevent IRS Collection Actions: As long as you comply with the terms of your agreement, the IRS will not pursue collection actions such as levies or liens, which can severely impact your credit or seize your assets.
- Simplified Process for Some Agreements: For smaller debts, the streamlined process makes it relatively easy to set up an IA without extensive documentation, saving you time and effort.[97]
- Risks:
- Interest and Penalties Accumulate: While an Installment Agreement allows you to pay off your debt over time, the unpaid balance will continue to accrue interest and penalties. This means the longer you take to pay off your debt, the more you'll ultimately owe. It's essential to

---

[97] https://www.albertsjohnsoncpa.com/?gad_source=1&gclid=CjwKCAiAxKy5BhBbEiwAYiW--7802NY-6yXEjodxVcPhjYhFLdUs1oaCx7yv8e16luY5HIUqtg0m3hoCDi0QAvD_BwE

factor in these additional costs when deciding how much to pay each month.

- Impact on Financial Health: If your financial situation changes and you cannot make the agreed-upon payments, you risk defaulting on your agreement. This could result in the IRS reinstating collection actions or terminating the contract altogether, leading to more severe consequences.

As an expert, I strongly advise against underestimating the long-term costs of an IA. Developing a strategic financial plan is the key to minimizing the total amount you'll pay. If possible, aim to pay more than the minimum monthly amount and resolve the debt as quickly as your finances allow.

Installment Agreements provide a valuable option for taxpayers facing significant debt but require careful consideration and planning. Whether you're opting for a streamlined agreement or navigating the complexities of a partial payment plan, the expertise of a tax professional can help ensure that you choose the best path for your financial future.

The Role of Tax Professionals in IAs

Regarding Installment Agreements, you might think the process is as simple as filling out a form and waiting for approval. However, the truth is that successfully navigating the IRS's requirements often involves much more than just submitting paperwork. A tax professional is crucial in ensuring you qualify for an Installment Agreement and secure the most favorable terms possible.

First, a tax professional will assess your financial situation in detail. They will look at your income, expenses, assets, and liabilities. This assessment is critical because it determines which type of Installment Agreement you qualify for and how much you'll be able to pay each month without straining your finances.

By taking a comprehensive view of your financial standing, a tax professional can help you avoid common pitfalls like agreeing to monthly payments that are too high, which could lead to defaulting on the agreement later.[98]

One of the most valuable aspects of having a tax professional on your side is their ability to streamline the entire process. They know exactly what documentation the IRS expects and can help you gather and organize all the necessary information before submitting your application. This attention to detail can significantly reduce the chances of delays or rejections caused by incomplete or inaccurate paperwork. For instance, submitting Form 9465 for an Installment Agreement might seem straightforward. Still, if your debt exceeds $50,000, you must submit Form 433-F (Collection Information Statement) to demonstrate your ability to pay. A tax professional will ensure that these forms are filled out accurately and completely, reducing the risk of your application being delayed or denied.[99]

Let me share a real-world example of how tax professionals can make a significant difference. Take the case of a small business owner I worked with who owed over $75,000 in back taxes. Initially, he tried to negotiate an Installment Agreement independently but was overwhelmed by the IRS's requests for additional documentation. By the time he reached out to me, he was on the verge of defaulting. After reviewing his financials, I determined that a Partial Payment Installment Agreement (PPIA) better fit his situation. We provided the necessary documentation to support his case, and he secured a manageable payment plan that not only kept his business afloat but also allowed him to gradually pay off his debt without accruing overwhelming interest and penalties.

---

[98] https://www.irs.gov/newsroom/resources-to-help-you-prepare-your-tax-return-and-resolve-tax-disputes

[99] https://www.irs.gov/payments/get-help-with-tax-debt

In another case, a single mother with a modest income faced nearly $30,000 in tax debt. She had been making minimum payments but found it increasingly difficult to keep up. After thoroughly reviewing her finances, I recommended a Streamlined Installment Agreement, which didn't require extensive financial documentation. I allowed her to spread her payments over a more extended period. This reduced her monthly payment significantly, giving her some much-needed breathing room to manage her household expenses.

In both scenarios, the involvement of a tax professional transformed what could have been a stressful and financially crippling situation into a manageable one. The key takeaway is that a tax professional doesn't just help with the paperwork; they also use their expertise to negotiate truly sustainable terms for you. By having a professional evaluate your financial situation and guide you through the process, you significantly increase your chances of securing an Installment Agreement that works in your favor.

Offer in Compromise (OIC): Settling Tax Debt for Less

When faced with a tax debt you cannot pay in full, the IRS offers a powerful option known as an Offer in Compromise (OIC). This program is designed specifically for those unable to meet their tax obligations due to financial hardship. As an expert in tax matters, I can tell you that navigating the OIC process can be complex, but when handled correctly, it can result in settling your tax debt for far less than the original amount owed.

What is an Offer in Compromise?

At its core, an Offer in Compromise is a settlement agreement between you and the IRS, where you agree to pay a reduced amount of your total tax liability. The IRS considers this option when it believes that collecting the total debt is unlikely or requiring a full payment would create an undue financial burden on the taxpayer. It allows taxpayers like yourself to resolve your outstanding tax debt for less than the total amount owed, provided you can prove that paying the total debt would be unrealistic based on your current financial situation.[100]

The key concept here is financial hardship. The IRS understands that, in some cases, collecting the total tax debt could force individuals into severe economic distress, leaving them unable to meet basic living expenses. In such cases, the OIC is intended to provide a reasonable solution for both parties. You get relief from overwhelming debt, and the IRS collects what it realistically can.

Eligibility Criteria for an OIC

- Before applying for an OIC, it's crucial to understand that not everyone qualifies. The IRS has strict criteria to determine eligibility, and financial hardship is the most critical factor. Here's what the IRS typically evaluates when considering whether to accept an offer:
- **Ability to Pay**: The IRS will assess your current and projected ability to pay off your debt based on your income, expenses, and assets. If it's clear that paying the total amount would leave you with insufficient resources for basic living expenses, you may be eligible for an OIC.
- **Income**: Your income level significantly influences the IRS's decision. If your earnings are low or unstable, the IRS may consider a settlement more appropriate. However, if your income indicates you could pay off the debt over time, you might not qualify for the OIC program.
- **Expenses**: The IRS reviews your necessary living expenses, including housing, utilities, food, and

[100] https://www.irs.gov/newsroom/the-what-ifs-for-struggling-taxpayers

transportation, to ensure that paying the tax debt would not push you below acceptable living standards. Demonstrating that your expenses leave little room for debt repayment is crucial in establishing eligibility.

- **Asset Equity**: The IRS will also look at the value of your assets, such as your home, car, savings, or investments. If you have significant equity in assets, the IRS might expect you to liquidate them to cover your tax liability before considering an OIC.
- To qualify, you must convince the IRS that it's more likely to collect a reduced amount than the total debt based on your financial circumstances. From my experience, this can be a complex task, and having a tax professional assess your situation can significantly improve your chances of success.[101]

The OIC Application Process

Applying for an Offer in Compromise is not a simple process—it requires detailed financial documentation and adherence to specific IRS guidelines. The IRS will scrutinize your financial situation, and missing any part of the application process can result in a rejection. Let's walk through the critical steps involved.

The first step in the process is submitting **Form 656 (Offer in Compromise)**, where you propose the amount you are willing to pay to settle your tax debt. You'll also need to include **Form 433-A (OIC)** or **Form 433-B (OIC)**, depending on whether you are an individual or a business. These forms provide a detailed overview of your financial situation, including income, assets, expenses, and liabilities. Be prepared to gather extensive financial records, such as pay stubs, bank statements, and mortgage or

---

[101] https://www.irs.gov/newsroom/things-to-remember-when-filing-2023-tax-returns

rental agreements, as you'll need to present a complete picture of your finances.

The application also requires an upfront application fee and an initial payment toward your offer. This payment can be substantial, depending on the size of your offer, and it's critical to ensure that your financial disclosure is accurate and complete. Any discrepancies or missing information could result in delays or outright rejection of your offer.

It's important to note that submitting an OIC doesn't automatically stop the IRS from taking collection actions. However, once your offer is under consideration, the IRS generally suspends collection efforts, giving you some breathing room while your case is evaluated.

Benefits and Drawbacks of an OIC

Securing an Offer in Compromise has clear advantages, but it is equally important to weigh the risks and obligations that come with it.

- Benefits:
- Settle for Less: The most obvious advantage is that you can settle your tax debt for a fraction of what you owe. This can be a financial lifeline for individuals struggling with insurmountable debt.
- Protection from Collection Actions: Once the IRS accepts your offer, you are protected from future collection actions, such as liens or levies on your property. This provides much-needed relief from the fear of losing your assets.
- Fresh Start: An accepted OIC allows you to move forward without the burden of lingering tax debt. For many, this provides a fresh start and the ability to regain control of their financial lives.
- Drawbacks:

- Upfront Costs: Even though you're settling for less, the application still has upfront costs, including fees and initial payments. These amounts can be challenging to come up with, particularly for individuals already in financial hardship.
- Ongoing Compliance: One of the critical conditions of an accepted OIC is that you must comply with all tax filing and payment requirements for five years after accepting your offer. Failure to meet this condition could result in the OIC being revoked, leaving you responsible for the original debt.
- Lengthy Process: The OIC process can be long and uncertain. The IRS may take months or even longer to review and decide on your offer. During this time, interest and penalties on your tax debt may continue to accrue, increasing the total amount you owe if your offer is not accepted.

From my professional experience, it's essential to carefully evaluate whether the OIC is the right path for you. The OIC can be invaluable if you face significant financial hardship and cannot see a feasible way to pay your total tax liability. However, the risks of non-compliance and the possibility of rejection mean it's not a decision to take lightly.[102]

In conclusion, while the Offer in Compromise provides an opportunity to settle tax debt for less, it requires careful preparation, thorough documentation, and a clear understanding of the risks involved. Working with a tax professional to evaluate your eligibility and navigate the application process is the best way to increase your chances of securing this relief.

---

[102] https://www.usa.gov/resolve-tax-disputes

The Role of Tax Professionals in the OIC Process

Navigating the Offer in Compromise (OIC) process is complex and requires precise financial disclosure and understanding of IRS guidelines. As a tax professional with years of experience, I can tell you that one of the most significant advantages you can have is expert guidance throughout this process. While it is possible to apply for an OIC on your own, the likelihood of success dramatically increases when a tax professional is involved. Here's why.

A tax professional's primary role in the OIC process is to increase your chances of approval by presenting a comprehensive and accurate picture of your financial situation. The IRS is looking for detailed information on your ability to pay, expenses, income, and assets, as well as any discrepancies or missing documentation that can lead to delays or rejections. As your representative, I ensure that your forms, mainly **Form 656** (Offer in Compromise) and **Form 433-A or 433-B**, are completed accurately and that all supporting documents are organized and included.[103]

The first step in the OIC process involves gathering the correct documentation. This includes a deep dive into your financial situation: pay stubs, bank statements, mortgage documents, utility bills, and more. A tax professional will review your entire financial profile and identify areas where you may be eligible for relief. By understanding what the IRS values most when assessing an OIC application, we can tailor your submission to reflect the most robust case for financial hardship.

Next, a tax professional conducts a detailed financial assessment. This is where our expertise shines. We analyze your income, expenses, and asset equity, ensuring we present an honest

---

[103] https://www.irs.gov/payments/pay-as-you-go-so-you-wont-owe-a-guide-to-withholding-estimated-taxes-and-ways-to-avoid-the-estimated-tax-penalty

yet favorable economic situation. For example, we know how to account for necessary living expenses in a way that demonstrates your limited ability to pay while ensuring all legal allowances are considered.

Negotiation with the IRS is another critical aspect. Once the IRS reviews your submission, they may question or seek clarification on your financial situation. Here, having a tax professional can make all the difference. We are well-versed in the IRS's processes and can negotiate effectively on your behalf. This is particularly important in complex cases where the IRS may initially reject the offer. We can appeal or adjust the offer with professional representation to ensure it meets your needs and the IRS's requirements.

Here are a few examples of how professional intervention led to successful OIC settlements. In one case, I represented a single mother overwhelmed by nearly $40,000 in tax debt. After carefully reviewing her finances, I submitted an OIC offering to settle for under $5,000. Her offer was accepted, relieving her of years of debt and financial strain.

In another case, a small business owner faced over $80,000 in tax liabilities. By organizing his financial records and negotiating with the IRS, I reduced his debt by nearly half, securing a manageable payment plan that allowed him to continue operating his business without fear of closure.

A tax professional increases your chances of OIC approval and provides peace of mind, knowing that[104]Every step is handled with precision and knowledge to reach a favorable outcome.

---

[104] https://www.usa.gov/file-taxes

When to Choose Installment Agreements vs. Offer in Compromise

As a taxpayer faced with overwhelming debt, one of the most important decisions you will make is choosing the proper method to resolve your financial obligations. The two most common IRS programs designed to help taxpayers in your position are Installment Agreements (IAs) and Offers in Compromise (OICs). Each solution has distinct advantages, but selecting the right one depends largely on your current financial situation, ability to pay, and long-term financial goals. In this section, I'll guide you through the key differences between these options and offer advice on which might be more appropriate.

Comparative Analysis: Installment Agreements vs. Offer in Compromise

An Installment Agreement allows you to pay off your tax debt over time by making monthly payments to the IRS. It's a flexible solution that enables taxpayers who can't pay their entire debt immediately to break it into manageable installments. On the other hand, an Offer in Compromise is designed for taxpayers who genuinely cannot pay their total tax liability. The OIC allows you to settle your debt for less than the total amount owed, but you must prove that paying the entire balance would cause undue financial hardship.

When deciding between an IA and an OIC, the first question you need to ask yourself is: "Can I reasonably pay off my tax debt over time, or is my financial situation so dire that I'll never be able to pay the full amount?"

Installment Agreements are ideal for taxpayers with a steady income who need time to pay off their debt but can realistically manage monthly payments.[105] For example, an IA might be your best route if you have consistent wages or business income. The IRS offers different types of Installment Agreements, including streamlined agreements that don't require extensive financial documentation for debts under $50,000. If your income is stable and you can commit to paying off the debt within a set period (usually up to 72 months), an IA provides a straightforward solution.

On the other hand, Offer in Compromise is designed for those in significant financial distress. If your income is low, your expenses exceed your income, or your assets are insufficient to cover your tax liability, an OIC may be more appropriate. For example, if you are unemployed, underemployed, or facing significant medical bills, the OIC could allow you to settle your debt for less than what you owe. However, the OIC process is more rigorous, requiring detailed financial disclosure to prove you cannot pay the total balance.

When to Choose an Installment Agreement

- An Installment Agreement is most appropriate if:
- You have a steady income or cash flow and can afford to make monthly payments without causing severe financial strain.
- You want to avoid collection actions, such as wage garnishments or liens, and are confident you can pay off the debt in full over time.
- Your total tax debt is under $50,000 (for streamlined IAs), or you can provide the necessary financial documentation for more significant debts.

One of the advantages of an IA is that it doesn't require you to liquidate assets to pay off your debt. If you have significant

---

[105] https://www.irs.gov/newsroom/what-if-i-cant-resolve-my-tax-problem-with-the-irs

equity in a home or other property, an IA allows you to keep your assets while making manageable payments to settle your tax liability.

However, you should be aware that while an IA prevents immediate collection actions, interest and penalties will continue to accrue on your unpaid balance. Therefore, the longer you take to pay off your debt, the more you will ultimately owe.[106] If possible, I always recommend paying more than the minimum monthly payment to reduce the total interest you will pay over time.

When to Choose an Offer in Compromise

- An OIC is a better choice if:
- Your financial situation is so dire that you will never realistically be able to pay off the total amount of your debt.
- You can demonstrate to the IRS that paying the total amount would create undue financial hardship.
- You have little to no disposable income after accounting for necessary living expenses, and your assets are minimal or not easily liquidated.

The OIC process is more complex than an IA and requires thorough documentation to prove your financial hardship. The IRS looks at factors such as your income, expenses, and equity in assets. If approved, an OIC can drastically reduce your debt, allowing you to settle for a fraction of what you owe. However, it's important to note that once the OIC is accepted, you must

---

[106] https://richardsonwealth.com/wealthstrategies/estateplanning/2024-year-end-tax-planning-checklist/?utm_source=Google&utm_medium=20303&utm_campaign=1923013&gad_source=1&gclid=CjwKCAiAxKy5BhBbEiwAYiW--9LhnSciki8mWdlqWgetIhvo5z5vBXO6V5nQ2dmXNLAJB-BxtznxzBoCr5QQAvD_BwE

comply with all tax filing and payment requirements for the next five years. Failure to comply can result in the IRS reinstating your total tax liability.

Long-Term Financial Planning with IAs and OICs

From a long-term financial planning perspective, both options require careful consideration. An Installment Agreement allows you to manage your debt over time without significantly disrupting your financial life. Still, the cost of accrued interest means it's best to pay off your debt as quickly as possible. While potentially considerably reducing your overall tax liability, an OIC requires more thorough documentation and compliance to avoid future complications.

As an expert, I advise consulting with a tax professional before making decisions. Whether you choose an IA or an OIC, the key is to select the option that best aligns with your financial situation and long-term goals. Managing tax debt is never easy, but you can regain control and work toward economic stability with the right strategy.

Navigating the Path to Financial Stability

When faced with tax debt, it's easy to feel overwhelmed and unsure how to proceed. As discussed, the IRS offers several solutions, including Installment Agreements and Offers in Compromise, to help you resolve your tax issues. The key is understanding which option best fits your financial situation and taking the necessary steps to apply it correctly.

Throughout this chapter, I've emphasized the importance of knowing your tax relief options and how they can be lifelines in times of financial hardship. Whether you choose an Installment Agreement to pay off your debt over time or pursue an Offer in Compromise to settle for less than the total amount, the goal is to regain control of your financial future. These tools can help you avoid more drastic consequences like wage garnishments or liens, which could further jeopardize your financial stability.[107]

However, the complexity of tax regulations and IRS procedures cannot be overstated. This is where professional tax support becomes invaluable. As mentioned, a tax professional can guide you through each step, from assessing your financial situation to submitting forms and negotiating with the IRS. By leveraging their expertise, you increase your chances of success and ensure that you are fully compliant with IRS rules, avoiding potential pitfalls that could lead to the rejection of your offer.

I've seen firsthand how proactive steps can lead to positive outcomes. You can resolve your tax debt, restore your financial health, and move forward with peace of mind by taking action now. Ignoring the problem only worsens it, while taking the proper steps today sets you on a path toward financial stability.[108]

Lastly, understanding your options and seeking professional guidance are the keys to overcoming tax debt and securing a better financial future. Whether dealing with substantial tax liabilities or trying to prevent future issues, the right strategy can help you regain control. So, don't wait—take that first step toward resolving your tax issues today.

---

[107] https://rtg.tax/tax-resolution/?gad_source=1&gclid=CjwKCAiAxKy5BhBbEiwAYiW--1VWLTELrVh-DjR8SCGFvpOOYSxpUbkuPyzsNlcUZRVRKlrd-BSNFRoCPd4QAvD_BwE

[108] https://www.irs.gov/individuals/get-ready-to-file-your-taxes

Conclusion: Be on Track… Always!

Complexity of Tax Laws and Regulations

Navigating the intricate web of tax laws in the United States can be overwhelming for individuals and businesses. As an expert in the field, I can confidently tell you that tax regulations are complex and change frequently, making it challenging to stay on top of the latest developments. Misunderstanding or overlooking even a tiny rule can be costly regarding penalties and lost opportunities for deductions or credits.

Thousands of pages of laws, guidelines, and interpretations govern the U.S. tax system. These cover everything from personal income to corporate taxation, estate taxes, and even specific industry regulations. For instance, there are distinct tax regulations for real estate, investment income, and international transactions. Tax laws are further complicated because they vary from state to state. This becomes an even more significant challenge for businesses operating in multiple states.

One key point to understand is that tax laws evolve constantly. Recent legislation, such as the Tax Cuts and Jobs Act (TCJA) of 2017, significantly changed individual and corporate tax rates, deductions, and credits. If you aren't keeping up with these changes—and let's be honest, most people don't have the time or expertise to do so—it's easy to miss out on opportunities or make errors that can result in financial repercussions.

Consider how the TCJA impacted deductions for home offices, a critical area for many remote workers and small business owners. Before 2017, the home office deduction was more straightforward, but recent changes introduced new criteria that can confuse those without specialized knowledge. Many taxpayers are unaware they could be missing out on significant deductions simply because they know how the law has shifted.

Another example is the expansion of tax credits for renewable energy investments, which benefit individuals and corporations. Many businesses are eager to take advantage of these credits. Still, they risk non-compliance or leaving money on the table without understanding the specific qualifications and reporting requirements.

Staying updated on these tax codes is not just advisable—it's essential. As an expert, I continuously review tax law updates, court rulings, and IRS notices. This ensures that I can provide accurate, timely advice to my clients, ensuring they remain compliant while optimizing their financial outcomes. Tax professionals like me use tools, databases, and direct communication with the IRS to stay ahead of the curve. Without this expertise, navigating the ever-changing landscape of U.S. taxation is nearly impossible.

The IRS has also become increasingly vigilant in enforcing tax compliance, especially for high-income individuals and businesses. For example, the crackdown on offshore accounts and the tightening of international tax rules have left many companies struggling to comply. Mistakes in this area can lead to severe penalties, including back taxes, interest, and audits. An expert understanding of tax law's domestic and international implications is indispensable.

Ultimately, the complexity of U.S. tax law cannot be underestimated. It's no longer just about filing your return and hoping for the best; it's about understanding evolving regulations' strategic opportunities and pitfalls. Whether you're an individual with a complicated financial situation or a business looking to maximize your deductions while remaining compliant, hiring a tax professional is not just recommended; it's essential.

Time and Efficiency

When filing taxes, time is often one of the most underestimated costs. Tax preparation isn't just about gathering documents and filling out forms; it's a time-consuming process that involves understanding laws, finding the correct deductions, and ensuring everything is filed correctly. As a tax professional, I've seen countless individuals and businesses waste valuable hours—and sometimes days—struggling through this process independently, only to find that they've made costly errors or missed opportunities to reduce their tax liability.

Hiring a tax professional saves you time and ensures efficiency, allowing you to focus on what truly matters—running your business, managing your career, or spending time with your family. Many people underestimate how long it can take to file a tax return correctly. For example, the IRS estimates that the average individual spends around 13 hours on tax preparation each year. This number can easily double or triple for business owners or those with more complicated finances.

The value of working with a tax expert is that we have a structured, streamlined system. We manage multiple clients, complex financial records, and varied tax scenarios efficiently because we do it daily. I have access to software, databases, and industry-specific knowledge that allow me to quickly identify deductions, apply credits, and ensure that every form is filled out accurately. What might take you hours of research, guesswork, and trial and error, I can handle it efficiently, thanks to my experience and tools.

Another benefit of working with a professional is that we handle the administrative side of things. Filing tax forms can be tedious, especially if you're unfamiliar with the deadlines, forms, and schedules required. I handle these details for my clients, ensuring all documentation is completed on time and submitted to the IRS without errors. This minimizes the risk of having your return rejected or delayed due to minor mistakes.

Moreover, in cases where clients have more complex financial portfolios—such as multiple income sources, investments, or properties—the process becomes even more time-consuming. In such cases, I manage all aspects of the tax filing process, from gathering documents to liaising with the IRS if necessary. This efficiency is critical, particularly for business owners, freelancers, and investors who cannot afford to lose valuable hours on administrative tasks.

Beyond just saving time, tax professionals ensure that your return is as optimized as possible. It's not uncommon for taxpayers to miss deductions, credits, or other opportunities simply because they aren't aware of them. By working with a professional, you're not only saving time but also potentially saving thousands of dollars. My job is to find every advantage available within the tax code and ensure you take full advantage of them without sacrificing compliance. The efficiency that comes from hiring a tax professional is unmatched. You can rest assured that your taxes are handled accurately and promptly while focusing on your best interests.

Expertise and Specialized Knowledge

One of the most important aspects to consider when managing taxes is the specialized knowledge tax professionals bring. Whether dealing with an enrolled agent, a CPA, or a tax attorney, each professional deeply understands tax law and its intricacies—far beyond what the average taxpayer can grasp. Their expertise is not just about filling out forms or submitting returns; it's about making informed decisions that can significantly impact your financial situation.

One of the primary areas where specialized knowledge is crucial is during an IRS audit. Audits are intimidating, and navigating them without professional guidance is risky. The IRS audit process involves reviewing your financial records in great detail, and the outcome can lead to penalties, additional taxes, or even legal consequences. As a tax professional, I help clients by reviewing their records, identifying potential red flags, and ensuring that their responses to the IRS are accurate and well-documented. With the proper representation, an audit can be resolved efficiently, often without further penalties.

Another situation where expertise is invaluable is when negotiating with the IRS. Whether you owe back taxes, deal with penalties, or seek an installment agreement, understanding how to approach the IRS is critical. Tax professionals have experience negotiating favorable terms for their clients, terms most individuals couldn't secure independently. For example, suppose you are facing a large tax bill you cannot pay immediately. In that case, I can assist in negotiating an installment agreement or an offer in compromise, allowing you to settle your debt for less than the total amount owed.

Filing complex tax returns is another area where tax professionals prove their worth. Not every tax return is a simple matter of reporting wages and a few deductions. When you're dealing with multiple income streams, investment portfolios, real estate transactions, or business income, the complexity of your return increases exponentially. As an expert, I can identify potential issues before they arise, ensuring that your tax return complies with all applicable laws and regulations. Moreover, I can help you plan for future tax liabilities, reducing your tax burden in the long run.

Many taxpayers also know the different filing statuses and tax strategies available. For instance, if you're a small business owner, your decision to file as a sole proprietor, an LLC, or an S-Corporation can significantly impact your tax obligations. Each entity type has its own rules and benefits, and knowing which option is best for your situation requires a deep understanding of tax law and financial planning. My role as a tax professional is to guide you through these decisions, helping you choose the most beneficial structure for your personal and business needs.

Tax laws are incredibly detailed, and the consequences of misunderstanding or misapplying them can be severe. Tax professionals like myself invest years in education, continuing professional development, and staying updated on the latest changes in tax law. This ongoing commitment allows us to serve our clients effectively, reducing their tax liabilities, protecting them from penalties, and ensuring compliance. When you hire a tax professional, you're not just paying for a service. You're investing in peace of mind, knowing that your financial matters are in expert hands.

Maximizing Deductions and Credits

One of the most significant advantages of working with a tax professional is maximizing your deductions and credits. Every taxpayer wants to reduce tax liability, but many miss out on substantial savings simply because they don't know where to look. My job as a tax expert is to ensure that no deduction or credit is overlooked and that you take full advantage of the available opportunities.

Let's start with deductions. Deductions reduce your taxable income, which means you pay less in taxes. However, identifying the proper deductions can be tricky. For instance, taxpayers often miss or incorrectly calculate home office deductions. If you work from home, I can help you determine whether you qualify for the home office deduction and how to calculate it correctly. This includes direct expenses, such as office supplies and a portion of your mortgage or rent, utilities, and internet costs.

Another common area where deductions are overlooked is charitable contributions. Many people donate to charities but fail to document these donations properly for tax purposes. As your tax professional, I ensure that you maximize your charitable deductions by keeping track of all eligible contributions and providing guidance on how to document them correctly. This can significantly affect your tax return, especially for individuals who donate regularly or make substantial contributions.

Now, let's talk about tax credits, which are even more valuable than deductions because they directly reduce the tax you owe. There are numerous credits available, but they vary depending on your situation. For example, the Earned Income Tax Credit (EITC) is a substantial benefit for low- to moderate-income families, but many eligible taxpayers either don't claim it or don't realize they qualify. I can help identify whether you meet the criteria for the EITC and ensure that you receive the total amount you're entitled to.

Similarly, education credits like the American Opportunity Tax Credit and the Lifetime Learning Credit can provide significant tax relief for students or parents paying for higher education. These credits can reduce your tax bill by thousands of dollars, but navigating the qualifications and application process can be challenging without professional help.

Finally, maximizing deductions related to business expenses—such as travel, meals, and depreciation—can lead to substantial tax savings for business owners. As a tax expert, I help business owners identify every possible deduction, ensuring their business expenses are properly categorized and documented for maximum tax benefit. Maximizing deductions and credits is not just about saving a few dollars here and there—it can profoundly impact your overall tax liability. With the guidance of a tax professional, you can ensure that you're taking full advantage of every opportunity the tax code offers.

Reducing the Risk of Errors and Audits

Filing taxes can be daunting, and even minor errors can have significant consequences. As a tax professional, I've seen firsthand how minor mistakes on tax returns can lead to costly penalties, delays, or even trigger an IRS audit. While often unintentional, these errors occur frequently when individuals attempt to navigate the complex tax system independently.

One of the most common mistakes is simple misreporting—entering the wrong income figure, mistyping Social Security numbers, or failing to include all forms of income. It's easy to overlook a freelance gig or a second job, but the IRS doesn't. You could face fines or an audit if your reported income doesn't match their records. Additionally, mistakes in applying for deductions, such as claiming ineligible expenses or overestimating amounts, can raise red flags with the IRS.

Filing without professional help also increases the likelihood of missing deadlines or using incorrect tax forms, which can lead to penalties. Even the slightest oversight, like neglecting to sign your return, can cause delays and complications. A tax professional mitigates these risks by meticulously reviewing your return, ensuring all income is reported accurately, and verifying that the proper forms and deductions are applied.

The danger of an IRS audit also arises when your return contains errors. While audits are rare, they become more likely when discrepancies or unusual claims don't align with the taxpayer's profile. As an expert, I know what the IRS looks for, and I can help ensure that your return is error-free, significantly reducing your risk of being audited. A tax professional's precision and expertise help avoid costly mistakes, minimize the risk of penalties, and ensure your return passes IRS scrutiny without issues.

Keeping Up with Changes

Tax laws in the United States change frequently—sometimes with significant reforms, other times through minor, less-publicized updates. For the average taxpayer, staying on top of these changes is not just tricky; it's nearly impossible. This is where the expertise of a tax professional becomes invaluable.

As a tax expert, it's my responsibility to stay informed about the latest changes in tax law. I constantly monitor legislative updates, IRS notices, and court rulings to ensure my clients are always compliant. These changes can significantly impact your tax return, from new tax credits to adjustments in deduction eligibility. Missing out on new opportunities or failing to comply with revised regulations can lead to penalties or missed savings.

For instance, the Tax Cuts and Jobs Act of 2017 brought sweeping changes that affected nearly every taxpayer in the U.S., from altering personal deductions to changing corporate tax rates. You may have missed valuable benefits if you didn't adjust your filing strategies in response to these changes. Since then, additional adjustments have been made to provisions for business expenses, healthcare credits, and investment gains. Without a professional to navigate these updates, making mistakes can easily cost you money or lead to compliance issues.

Tax professionals like me also anticipate upcoming changes. This proactive approach lets you adjust your financial planning in advance rather than reacting to new rules afterward. For example, suppose Congress passes a law increasing tax rates for specific income brackets. In that case, I can help you strategize to minimize the impact on your finances, perhaps by making early withdrawals or investments.

Keeping up with tax law changes is a full-time job, and tax professionals are equipped to handle it. By staying informed and applying this knowledge to your situation, I ensure you are always compliant, up to date, and taking full advantage of new opportunities in the tax code.

Handling Complex Financial Situations

Managing taxes can quickly become overwhelming for individuals with more complicated financial portfolios—such as business owners, investors, or those with multiple income streams. A simple oversight could cost you significantly in penalties or missed opportunities when dealing with various income sources, deductions, and credits. That's where tax professionals like myself come in. We are trained to navigate the intricacies of complex financial situations, ensuring that you remain compliant with tax laws while optimizing your financial outcomes.

Consider, for example, a small business owner with investment properties and freelance income. These income streams require different reporting methods, deductions, and tax strategies. Attempting to manage this without professional help increases the risk of errors, such as misreporting income or missing eligible deductions, which could trigger an audit or lead to hefty penalties. As a tax expert, I understand the nuances of these financial landscapes and ensure that all aspects of your financial life are handled correctly and efficiently.

Tax professionals are also adept at working with individuals with complex international financial ties, such as foreign investments or earnings. In these cases, compliance with U.S. and international tax laws is critical to avoid double taxation or legal issues. With our specialized knowledge, we manage these complexities, ensuring you maximize your financial potential while fully complying with all regulations.

Strategic Tax Planning

Tax professionals do much more than file returns. One of our most valuable services is strategic tax planning, which is essential for minimizing your tax burden and setting yourself up for long-term financial success. Strategic tax planning isn't just about the current tax year—it's about thinking ahead, ensuring that every financial decision you make today is tax-efficient for years to come.

One key element of tax planning is retirement planning. How you save for retirement, whether through a 401(k), IRA, or other savings vehicles, can significantly impact your tax liabilities in the future. By working with a tax professional, you can structure your contributions to reduce your tax burden today while securing a more tax-efficient future. For instance, a Roth IRA may be ideal for those who expect to be in a higher tax bracket in retirement, as withdrawals from this account are tax-free. On the other hand, traditional IRAs offer tax deductions today, but withdrawals are taxed later. A tax professional helps determine the best strategy for you.

Another critical aspect of tax planning is investment strategy. Whether you're investing in stocks, bonds, real estate, or other assets, each investment decision has tax implications. By coordinating your investment choices with your overall tax strategy, you can minimize capital gains taxes and take advantage of tax-loss harvesting, where you sell securities at a loss to offset gains.

Lastly, estate planning is a crucial area where tax professionals can offer strategic advice. Properly structuring your estate ensures that your heirs aren't burdened with unnecessary taxes and that your assets are distributed according to your wishes. This includes planning for estate taxes, which can significantly reduce the value of your estate if not handled correctly. By working with a tax professional, you can implement strategies like gifting, trusts, and charitable donations to minimize the tax impact on your estate. Strategic tax planning is about looking beyond the immediate tax season and setting yourself up for financial success in the long term. With expert guidance, you can ensure that every aspect of your financial life works together to minimize taxes and maximize your wealth.

Peace of Mind and Stress Reduction

One of the most significant benefits of working with a tax professional is the peace of mind you gain. Taxes can be stressful, especially if you're unsure whether you've filed everything correctly or worried about potential audits or penalties. By entrusting your tax responsibilities to a professional, you alleviate that burden, allowing you to focus on what matters most in your personal or professional life.

The stress accompanying tax season is not just about the time it takes to gather documents and file returns. It's also about the fear of making a mistake. Whether it's missing a deadline, failing to report income accurately, or overlooking a deduction, when you work with a tax expert, you can know everything is handled correctly. We stay current on tax law changes, ensure that all your paperwork is in order, and verify that you're taking full advantage of all available deductions and credits.

Additionally, if you're ever faced with an IRS audit or other tax-related issues, having a professional on your side can dramatically reduce your anxiety. Tax professionals like myself have experience dealing with the IRS, and we know how to navigate the system to resolve issues quickly and effectively. You don't have to worry about dealing with the IRS alone—we handle that for you.

Ultimately, working with a tax professional isn't just about accuracy and compliance; it's about reducing the stress and mental load tax season can bring, ensuring you can move forward with confidence and peace of mind.

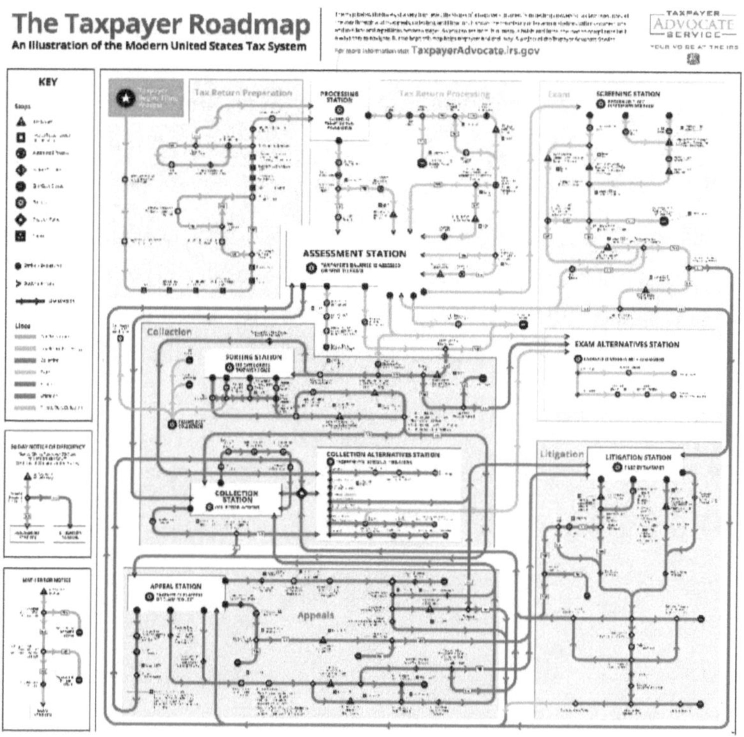

The Taxpayer Roadmap
An Illustration of the Modern United States Tax System
For more information visit TaxpayerAdvocate.irs.gov
TAXPAYER ADVOCATE SERVICE
KEY
Tax Return Preparation
PROCESSING STATION
Tax Return Processing
Exam
SCREENING STATION
ASSESSMENT STATION
Collection
SORTING STATION
EXAM ALTERNATIVES STATION
COLLECTION ALTERNATIVES STATION
COLLECTION STATION
Litigation
LITIGATION STATION
APPEAL STATION
Appeals

YOU ARE ENTITLED TO A FREE 30-MINUTE

TAX DEBT ANALYSIS ($137 Value) FOR PURCHASING THIS BOOK.

If you're reading this book, you or someone you know may face a tax issue. Concerns like potential jail time or the IRS seizing your home can be overwhelming. However, there is a solution. The first step to address your tax concerns can significantly improve your financial future.

Contact us for a free, confidential consultation at (http://DixsonAssociates.com) or call 888-684-4113 or 573-426-4824. If we're unavailable, please leave a message mentioning you've read this book, and we will return your call promptly.

LEGAL DISCLAIMER

While every effort has been made to ensure that the information in the book is correct as of the time of publication, tax laws and regulations are constantly changing.

This book is designed to provide accurate and authoritative information about the subject matter covered. Still, it is sold with the understanding that the publisher does not render legal or accounting services and that no information contained herein should be construed as legal advice.

If legal advice or other expert assistance is required, the services of a competent professional should be sought. The publisher does not guarantee or warrant that readers who use the information provided in this publication will achieve results similar to those discussed throughout the book.

About the Author

Felecia is an Enrolled Agent, Licensed to Practice before the IRS, a Certified Tax Representation Consultant, and an Accredited Tax Advisor. Felecia is an extraordinary individual whose diverse accomplishments span various fields. From a young age, her life has been marked by remarkable achievements that illustrate her multifaceted talents and dedication.

One of Felecia's early notable moments was performing for Disney at the opening ceremonies of the 10th Pan American Games. This event highlighted her artistic talents and set the stage for significant accomplishments in the entertainment industry.

Beyond her musical endeavors, Felecia has a unique talent for orchestrating large-scale events, including city-wide fireworks displays. These events require creativity, meticulous planning, and coordination, showcasing her ability to manage complex projects successfully. Her creative talents, however, do not overshadow her practical skills, as evidenced by her passion for the outdoors. She specifically substantiates fish tales with photographic evidence. This hobby illustrates her attention to detail and ability to combine leisure activities with precision and documentation.

Amidst these creative and recreational pursuits, Felecia has also garnered significant accolades in the field of accounting. Her professional achievements in accounting demonstrate her analytical skills and dedication to her work. Her affinity for mathematics, which began in her junior year of high school, has been a consistent thread throughout her life. She recalls how her interest in dismantling and reassembling objects naturally complemented her growing passion for math. For Felecia, mathematics is not just a subject but a lens through which she views the world. She believes that algebraic principles are integral to everyday life, helping solve equations to achieve desired outcomes.

Felecia's professional journey is marked by her involvement in several influential committees that underscore her commitment to improving the interface between IRS operations and taxpayer advocacy. She has served on the IRS Advisory Council (IRSAC), the Special Enrollment Exam Advisory Council (SEEC), and the Taxpayers Advocacy Panel (TAP). These roles highlight her taxation expertise and dedication to improving tax-related processes and policies. Her contributions in these capacities have significantly impacted how the IRS interacts with taxpayers, ensuring more efficient and taxpayer-friendly operations.

In addition to her professional and creative pursuits, Felecia remains deeply committed to her community. She serves as the Treasurer of the local Board for the Veterans Park Association Committee. This role allows her to give back to her community and support local initiatives, demonstrating her dedication to service and leadership abilities.

Felecia's story is one of remarkable versatility and dedication. Her accomplishments in the arts, accounting, community service, and her roles in influential committees illustrate a life driven by passion, creativity, and a commitment to excellence. Through her diverse talents and achievements, Felecia exemplifies how one can excel in multiple fields while making meaningful contributions to both professional and community spheres.

In summary, Felecia's life is a testament to the power of pursuing one's passions, embracing diverse interests, and positively impacting various domains. Her journey from performing at high-profile events to securing significant roles in professional and community organizations demonstrates a unique blend of creativity, analytical skills, and commitment to service.

Felecia's story inspires others to explore their multifaceted talents and strive for excellence in all endeavors.

www.ingramcontent.com/pod-product-compliance
Lightning Source LLC
LaVergne TN
LVHW090358210926
848480LV00002B/383